Guide To Small-Scale Property Development

And the Rise of the Landlord Developer

Other books by Ian Child and Ritchie Clapson

Industrial To Residential Conversions: The essential guide to converting industrial buildings for profit

Other books by Ian Child

Your Own Personal Time Machine: Get Your Life Back

Guide To Small-Scale Property Development

And the Rise of the Landlord Developer

Ian Child & Ritchie Clapson

 Equeum

Disclaimer

The authors and publisher have made every effort to ensure that the information contained in this book is accurate and correct at the time of publication, however they do not assume and hereby disclaim any liability to any party for any damages, loss (financial or otherwise) or disruption caused by any errors or omissions, howsoever such errors or omissions arose.

Any references to planning regulations, legal and accounting practices, options or considerations are given for information only and do not constitute legal or financial advice. Professional advice should always be sought from suitably qualified personnel who are familiar with your specific circumstances before making any decision that may affect your financial or legal position.

Published in Great Britain June 2022 by Equeum.

Facebook: propertyceotraining
Twitter: Property_CEO
Instagram: propertyceotraining
Website: www.propertyceo.co.uk
Show: www.propertyceo.co.uk/opendoor
Podcast: www.propertyceo.co.uk/podcasts

All profits from the sale of this book go to KidsOut, the fun and happiness children's charity, a fantastic cause that's very close to our hearts.

For more information on the amazing work that they do, please visit www.kidsout.org.uk.

Table of Contents

Acknowledgements

This book wouldn't have been possible without the support of the entire propertyCEO family.

From our incredible helpdesk staff, our operations team and our professional coaches right through to our amazing students whose life-changing journeys we are privileged to share, we're indebted to each of you for your support and friendship. You know who you are.

Whether you're teaching it or learning about it, property development can dramatically change your life for the better. But it's far more fun when you're sharing the journey with friends.

1. Introduction

What you will learn from this book

Property development has always been a subject of fascination for many people, and it's certainly got a lot to recommend it. The attraction of significant profits combined with the ready availability of opportunity and expertise means that there really are very few barriers to entry. Not surprisingly, then, the thought of taking on a small development project has occurred to many people at some time or another.

Interestingly, we've recently seen a surge in the number of people looking to take on small-scale property developments. Several things have driven this; people facing an uncertain financial future without a solid pension to rely on, the recent taxation and regulation changes in the buy-to-let sector that have hit landlords hard, business and career challenges in the wake of the combined recession and coronavirus pandemic. And, of course, some people simply want to change their financial situation for the better, ditch the day job, and start to lead a happier and more abundant life.

But while the rewards look enticing, most people are aware that the road to success will likely be littered with risks and complexities that could all too easily unseat the unwary traveller. It's true that, while the upside of doing development well can be life-changingly good, success is never guaranteed. And if you've never developed property before, you won't know where the pitfalls are.

So, where on earth should you start?

Well, we'd like to think that this book is a good place. Its purpose is to give you enough information to decide whether property development is a good fit for you and, if it is, how to go about doing it with the minimum risk and the maximum profitability. We'll be answering all those questions that most people have about property development, such as how it all works, where to find the money, how to build a team, how to find the best development projects and analyse them properly, and how to get credibility as a developer before you've even started developing. And, of course, we'll also suggest why you might want to choose property development over all the other exciting wealth-creation strategies there are out there.

We'll be looking at the current market opportunities and exploring the raft of new Permitted Development Rights that now allow a wide range of commercial properties to be converted to residential use without the need for full planning permission. The government is now actively encouraging people to get into small-scale property development, and we'll explain why they're doing this, but also how you can take full advantage of what's on offer.

We're also going to show you how to create a support infrastructure that will allow you to find the answer to almost any question that you could ever encounter in your development journey. That way, if you start a development project, you'll never get caught in the unenviable situation of thinking, 'what on earth should I do next?' or 'who can I turn to for help?'. We'll also describe the system we've developed that turns property development into a process that allows developers to follow prescribed steps through the entire end-to-end journey.

In the interest of balance, we should also tell you what this book doesn't cover. The most important point is that we won't be going into the procedural detail on exactly HOW to do a development. As you can imagine, there are lots of moving parts, and this isn't intended to be a manual or reference book. Believe us, that would be a volume many times the size of this one, and possibly not the lightest of reads either (even if we threw in some smiley faces ☺).

Our guidance will cover all forms of development and the risks and rewards involved with each. So, whether you're looking to convert an existing building or build something brand new from the ground up, the advice we'll give you will equally apply.

Finally, it would be remiss not to mention one key question that often comes up, namely 'do I need lots of my own money to develop property?'. The short answer is 'no'; in fact, you'll need significantly less than if you were buying a buy-to-let investment property. But taking on a project without any money whatsoever, while still possible, is trickier. Rest assured, we'll be covering all the bases when we tackle this subject later in the book. But for now, we're not going to be presuming you've got a king's ransom stashed away. You won't need endlessly deep pockets; in fact, you may be a little surprised when you see the numbers involved.

So, in summary, whatever your background, you'll have a pretty good idea about what's involved in becoming a successful small-scale property developer by the end of this book.

We've divided the book into four parts, as follows:

Part 1 – Why Choose Property Development?

Here we'll cover some of the basic principles of development and compare it to some other property investing strategies. Plus, we'll also give you a flavour of what's possible when you develop successfully, to really get your juices flowing.

Part 2 – What Should I Build?

In this section, we'll be looking at the range of development opportunities in the market today. We'll also be exploring the environment that a small-scale property developer must operate in and the rules that 'govern' the industry.

Part 3 – How Do I Become A Developer?

There are some common questions people always ask about property development, and this is where we answer them. Myths corrected, theories debunked, and a good overview of everything to do with credibility, deal finding, financing, team building, and making a profit.

Part 4 – Developing Your First Project

In this final part, we look at the skills you need to become a developer, what makes the best developers stand out from the rest of the pack, and the knowledge you need to get out of the blocks and on your way.

The final thing to mention before we kick things off is that while small-scale property development is easy to get into, it isn't easy to do (although, depending on your current understanding, it may be easier than you thought it was!). It requires hard work, knowledge, dedication, persistence, and an entrepreneurial spirit. There will be ups and downs along the journey, and there is risk involved, particularly for those who dive in without looking. But, on the plus side, it's creative, hugely rewarding, requires little technical knowledge, and can be done in your spare time, alongside a day job. And, of course, it can quite literally change your life.

There are no certain ways of making a fortune, yet small-scale property development is the surest way we've come across, when you do it right.

So, let's start by taking a look at what's possible.

Part 1

Why Choose
Property Development?

Ian Child & Ritchie Clapson

2. Some First Principles

Why should I listen to you?

In this chapter, we're going to kick things off with a few fundamentals to get us nicely warmed up and on the same page. And we thought we should start by telling you a bit about us, so you've got some confidence in the information we're giving you. After all, you'd be pretty miffed if you got to the end of the book and found out that we'd googled it all.

So, how do we know all this stuff (and why should you believe anything we tell you)? Well, to give you some background, the two of us met for the first time some years ago. Having retired from corporate life in his late forties, Ian was looking for someone to give him some one-to-one mentoring in property development, and he went along to an event where Ritchie was speaking. Ritchie had been in development for the best part of four decades, and as a qualified structural engineer, was the only industry professionally qualified property development trainer in the country. Having experienced the somewhat mixed quality of the training on offer elsewhere, Ian had been impressed with the glowing feedback from Ritchie's other students. He was also impressed that the company Ritchie had built was selected by the UK government as the peer review engineer for the London 2012 Olympic Stadium, Aquatics Centre, and Velodrome, and had also designed the famous

Wimbledon retracting roof. Not everyone has that on their CV, plus Ritchie had also worked on hundreds of less iconic projects, from new builds to conversions, both large and small. And it was the idea of doing small-scale developments that particularly interested Ian. At the time, office to residential conversions were just taking off, but Ian could see that there were opportunities that extended way beyond that.

Having worked with Ritchie for around a year, Ian found the training to be excellent, particularly how Ritchie had built a system around property development that made life a lot easier. Then, one evening over a beer, Ian put forward an idea. Why don't the two of them create a property development training company? After all, Ritchie could only train a handful of students one-to-one. But by digitising the training material and creating a coaching framework around it, many more people could benefit from Ritchie's knowledge and get into development. Ian knew how to create a training business, and Ritchie had the development knowledge and experience – surely it was a perfect combination?

Ritchie said he thought it was a terrible idea, possibly the worst idea Ian had ever had, which was saying something. But the more they talked about it, the more he started to be swayed until eventually, he began to think it was a brilliant idea after all and was extremely glad he'd thought of it.

There was another critical factor involved in creating propertyCEO. Both Ian and Ritchie knew from long experience that property knowledge on its own isn't much use if you don't also have the business skills to turn it into a successful enterprise. You also need to have the right mindset to overcome any hurdles, get out of your own way, and take action. Like any three-legged stool, it doesn't work if any legs are missing. And what would be the point of giving people property knowledge if they didn't also have the business and mindset skills to make it work? There were relatively few development training products on the market, and none offered all three elements. They typically focused exclusively on high-level property knowledge and omitted business skills and mindset altogether.

Luckily for propertyCEO, Ian and Ritchie had over 75 years of business experience between them that they could share with their students. Ian had previously run the multinational business arm of a private-equity-owned financial services company and had been responsible for delivering nine-figure annual top-line revenues working with some of the world's largest brands. And as a serial entrepreneur, Ritchie's experience included buying, growing, and selling his own businesses and advising SMEs on their own business strategy and preparing them for sale, as well as working as a non-executive advisor to numerous firms.

And when it came to the mindset leg of the stool, Ian had spent over a decade studying a wide range of personal development strategies. He'd also experienced first-hand the senior executive training used by private equity businesses to get the very best out of their management teams. By distilling this knowledge into its training, propertyCEO could give students the tools to avoid blockers that could stop them from achieving success.

Which, in a nutshell, was how propertyCEO came to be born. And, just a few short years later, with the help of some great people, it has grown to become the best property development training business of its type anywhere. Thousands of people have received propertyCEO's training during that time, although a much smaller number are invited onto its flagship 6-month Mentorship Programme. This isn't exclusivity for its own sake; the overarching principle of propertyCEO is for students to get results, not just to learn. By limiting the student intake, coaches can devote more time to each student, creating a community of new developers who are really going places.

The information in this book is based on the same systems and processes that we teach on our Mentorship Programme; however, the focus is very much on giving you the property knowledge; why should you consider development, and how can you do it successfully.

Why are we called propertyCEO? It's because we teach people how to develop property while playing the role of Chief Executive Officer (CEO) in their own development business. We don't want you to get your hands dirty on-site or to try to manage your own projects. We don't even want you to choose the curtains. Instead, you'll be using other people's money to pay someone to do all that work for you while you do something far more interesting instead. One of the biggest mistakes we come across is people thinking that property development needs to involve some sort of hands-on, day-to-day oversight by you, the developer. If you do it properly, you'll be outsourcing most of the work to people far better qualified than you while you take on the most senior management position of all, not to mention banking the lion's share of the profits. So, if a more hands-off approach to development sounds quite appealing, and you like to see other people doing most of the work while you're making most of the money, then you're definitely in the right place. But rest assured, there will still be plenty for you to do.

Right, that's enough about us. Let's move on to something far more exciting. There are lots of investment opportunities around, and property has a fantastic track record for being, in relative terms, as safe as houses. But once you've decided that property is a good investment strategy, there are still different options available to you, the two obvious ones being; do you choose to develop property, or do you become a buy-to-let landlord? Let's consider the pros and cons of each.

Property investment versus property development

We've started to see something of a renaissance in the world of property investment, to the extent that many property investors are now seeing development as a preferable strategy to the once favoured alternative of becoming a buy-to-let landlord.

A key reason has been a tax-grab by the UK Government on the rental sector over the past few years. Let's face it, landlords garner little public sympathy, and as a minority group, they are an obvious target for increased taxation since few votes will be lost. During the same period, there has also been a significant increase in the regulation that landlords must adhere to and an increase in the rights of tenants. While these regulatory changes have helped ensure the rental sector is fairer and safer, it's pushed many additional costs onto landlords. Coupled with other recent tax hikes, this hasn't only caused many landlords to sell up and leave the market; it has also dissuaded many prospective property investors from entering it.

Instead, the mantle of 'number one property strategy' seems to be heading in the direction of small-scale development. One of the reasons for this is arguably political; the government needs to build 300,000 new homes each year to find enough places for people to live. There are also many brownfield sites available in the UK, which are a key redevelopment target since the government understandably prefers existing property to be 'recycled' instead of building on greenfield land. However, most of these brownfield sites have little appeal for the major housebuilders because the plots are too small. They understandably don't get out of bed for less than a few million in profit. As a result, the government knows it must rely on small-scale developers to help them solve the problem. We'll be looking at exactly how they're encouraging this shortly, but while landlords are having a rough time of it, developers appear very much to be flavour of the month. And the apple of the government's eye, at least for now.

Landlord vs Developer

One of the things that has dissuaded many people from going down the development route has been its perceived level of complexity and risk compared with becoming a landlord. We're talking in general here about people who are not, at least initially, looking to become full-time landlords. They simply want to create a haven for their savings and perhaps create some 'passive' income along the way. After all, being a 'property developer' sounds more like a career or job title than an investment strategy, doesn't it? And lots of 'ordinary' people have the odd buy-to-let property that they've either invested in or inherited, so it feels like a more mainstream approach.

It's also easier to understand how being a landlord works. Buy a property, rent it out to some tenants, make a little profit from the rental income, and make even more profit from the equity growth over time. What's not to like or understand about that?

Well, the recent tax raid on landlords aside, there are some reasons why being a landlord isn't quite as passive or straightforward as many might think. The first and most important of these is dealing with tenants.

Tenants are human and therefore come pre-programmed with the full range of quirks associated with the species. Some are nice, decent, honest, and reliable, while others aren't. Some will pay rent on time, while others won't. Some will look after your property like it's their own, while others will treat it like an Ibiza rental car.

Also, landlords have a raft of significant legal responsibilities for the maintenance of their property and the safety of tenants. These same tenants also enjoy an increasing number of rights that are onerous on you, the landlord. Ultimately, tenants are often stressful, but unfortunately, you can't be a landlord without them. In contrast, developers don't have any tenants.

The other consideration you'll have as a landlord relates to the maintenance of your property. If the boiler goes bang, the shower goes pop, or a burst pipe floods the house, then you're on the hook for the costs involved in sorting them out. And these things will need sorting immediately as you've got tenants who have paid for the privilege of having a fully functioning house in which to live.

So, while the business model for owning rental property remains perfectly valid, it's not entirely passive, stress-free, or cost-free. While a property developer doesn't have to deal with tenants or broken boilers (everything is new, unused, and under warranty), they will have to deal with a completely different set of issues and expenses.

In short, the development model isn't 'better' than the rental model; they both have their risks, stresses, and costs. However, we think it's important to be transparent about what's involved in both so you can get a good perspective on how they stack up against each other. Plus, we'll also be looking at whether doing both could perhaps turn out to be the perfect strategy. But more on that later; first, we need to understand precisely what small-scale development means.

What is 'small-scale' development?

Development projects come in all shapes and sizes, from large housing estates and landmark commercial buildings at one end of the scale, right down to building a conservatory on your residential home at the other. Both involve creating value by developing property. The numbers involved are similarly diverse, with hundreds of millions at one end and a few thousand at the other. So, where on this spectrum would 'small-scale' development sit?

...e're not talking about building a conservatory or an ...ension on your house. Nor are we talking about buying a 'doer-upper' and flipping it on. There's absolutely nothing wrong with either, however they lack the scale we're looking for. We ideally want to be returning a six-figure profit from each development, i.e., a minimum of £100,000, and typically this would involve stepping up a notch on the development ladder.

As a developer, you should be looking to achieve a minimum 20% return (profit) based on your project's gross development value (GDV). The GDV is the value of the units you build, i.e., what they will sell for. Therefore, if you want to achieve a £100,000 profit, your GDV would need to be £500,000.

How many units will you be building? Well, let's assume that we were building 1-bed flats. If we took an average value of £125,000 per flat, it means we'd be building just four apartments to make £100k profit. Not exactly a massive development project, but certainly a different proposition to building an extension or refurbishing a house.

So, if four flats are the minimum, what would be the maximum? We think twenty units is probably the limit for what constitutes 'small-scale'. Using the same maths, a 20-unit development would give you a GDV of £2.5m, and a profit of £500k. Hopefully, this paints a picture of the scale of the projects we'll be considering in this book.

It's also worth noting that it's predominantly the number of units you're building rather than their value that determines a project's complexity. Four flats in London will have a higher GDV than the same flats in Leeds, yet their complexity may be similar. But as a guide, building between 4 and 20 units that produce £100k to £500k in profit is a fair indication of what constitutes small-scale development. If you're aiming for something bigger, then while we certainly won't put you off, we would highly recommend that your first project should be a smaller one. All those brand-new cogs and gears will be meshing together for the first time, so it makes sense to make your first deal as simple and low risk as possible, then step up once you have a successful project under your belt.

How long will it take to complete a small-scale development? In relative terms, these projects are completed quite quickly due to their lack of complexity. To be prudent, we usually work on a period of 18-24 months from start to finish for a conversion project, from when you first find your deal to when you bank the proceeds having sold your last unit. New build projects would typically take slightly longer. Less complex projects or projects that sell quickly could have shorter timescales. Equally, in a more challenging market, sales could take longer.

A word about build to rent

When developing property, you have a choice of either selling what you build and pocketing the profits (build to sell) or retaining ownership of the units and renting them out (build to rent). The majority of what we'll be covering in this book applies to both strategies, however where there's a particular nuance or consideration relating to either, we'll be sure to point it out.

Why small is beautiful

One of the more common problems we've seen with new developers is what we call 'expansion syndrome'. This is where people quite reasonably start with a small development project they manage to complete successfully. So, they decide their second project should be a bit bigger because twice the GDV doesn't equate to twice the work. For example, a £2m GDV project won't involve twice as much effort from the developer's point of view as a £1m GDV project, yet it should yield twice the profit. All very true, in theory at least.

Now there's nothing wrong with this approach in principle. As we said, start small, and then get a bit bigger once you have some experience. The problem comes when this expansion theory is applied with every development. So, after a £2m GDV project, they double up to a £4m project, and then an £8m project. Bear in mind that the developer would expect to make a 20% profit on these numbers; you can see the attraction. An £8m GDV project should return £1.6m in profit to the developer. Given that this sum is more than the average person earns in their entire lifetime, you might be thinking, 'what's not to like?'

But there's a problem with this approach, and it lies in the fact that more significant deals carry greater complexity and greater risk. They can also bring a great deal more stress for the developer. Each property development project is complex, and each has its unique challenges. As a result, you will encounter unique scenarios with your second project that you didn't experience on your first. Even experienced developers will face new challenges on their twentieth project, ones they've not seen before. A successful deal can therefore lure you into a false sense of security. "That last project went quite well," you'll think, and then assume that a bigger scheme should be well within your grasp.

You can probably see where this is heading. If a wheel were to fall off your development 'bus', you'd prefer it to happen when you're travelling slowly than when you're travelling at breakneck speed. We occasionally hear of developers who have crashed and burned on a large project. Their schemes kept getting larger and more complex until they encountered a problem or made a mistake on a large-scale development. The success of their previous projects created a false sense of security, and they realised too late that you could easily encounter a new challenge that can trip you up, even if you've plenty of experience.

So, how big should your development be? In our business, we speak to people looking to get into development daily, and one of the questions we ask them is what sort of profit they're looking to achieve from each development. The answers vary considerably, from people looking to earn seven figures to those for whom a modest £50k would be enough. However, the average is probably around £200k, which, using our 20% profit calculation, would equate to a GDV of £1m. You can do the math for the average flat cost in your area to work out how many flats you'd need to build to achieve whatever your target profit number is. The critical point is that these are not big projects; in fact, they are considered very small in development terms. And small is beautiful because it carries less risk and complexity, and the downside of a wheel falling off is far less damaging than on a larger development.

So, our best advice would be to keep things small, then simply rinse and repeat. Sure, you can take on more than one project, but make them both small-scale. In our experience, that's the best way to achieve the right balance of a life-changing income and as stress-free a life as possible.

Another good idea is to first take some time out to work out what income you need. All too often, we find that people have a notional target profit figure in their heads without having worked out what it is in life they want to do and, therefore, how much money they need to do it. You may find you need less money than you think, which in turn means you can do smaller, less-risky developments.

Types of development you can do

Development essentially falls into one of just two categories. The first is new build, and you won't be surprised to learn that this involves building a property from scratch. You'll typically be building on virgin land, where you'll have to dig the footings, lay the foundations, and then build from the ground up. Examples would include a back garden, a field, or a tract of land between or amongst existing properties.

The second type of development is called a conversion. This probably won't come as a complete shock either, but it's where you take an existing property and convert it into something else. For example, you might take an office building and convert it into residential flats. We would also include demolition in this category, i.e., where you knock something down and replace it with a brand-new building since you're technically converting the site, albeit not the existing building.

In either case, it's not a requirement that you create residential units, although usually, residential development will be the most profitable thing to build. However, you could equally build offices instead of houses, turn a retail unit into some office pods, or a gym into a restaurant, and so on. This can be a great idea in commercial or retail areas that are not best suited to residential homes.

Should you have a preference? Some developers like new build because they see it as a blank canvas. Once they're out of the ground, there's no existing infrastructure or constraints for them to contend with. However, we recommend that new developers go down the conversion route for their first project for three reasons. The first is that most of the problems developers encounter in their projects are typically in the ground. It might look like a benign square patch of grass that you're going to be building on, but you can't see what's under the surface. Once you start digging, all manner of horrors could be unearthed, such as utility pipes, power cables, old wells, watercourses, or a requirement for deeper foundations due to unstable soil. This isn't usually something you'll need to contend with on conversion projects, as you'll usually be keeping the existing foundations.

The second benefit of a conversion is ironically brought about by the constraints that new build developers are looking to avoid. Because we're converting an existing building, we can't physically build exactly what we'd like since we're forced to work around what's already there. Sure, we can knock down some internal walls, but our development is necessarily restricted by the footprint, height, and existing outer walls of our host building. This can give more enterprising developers an edge. If we can be the best at maximising that space based on the existing restrictions, then we'll make more profit. And if our profit projections are higher than less imaginative or less well-educated developers, then we'll be able to pay more for the building, which means we'll win the deal. So, what many developers think of as a disadvantage, turns out to be quite an advantage if you know your stuff.

The third and final reason for going down the conversion route is the ability to use something called Permitted Development Rights (PDRs). We'll be talking about these in detail later, but essentially, they give developers the right to change the use of a building without the need for full planning permission. This can significantly reduce the risk and timescales involved in a project, which is a big win for the developer. New build projects always require full planning permission, and, as we'll discover later, this can be a minefield.

Whatever your preference, the principles we'll be describing in this book, unless we state otherwise, will relate to both new build and conversions. As a training company, we train students to tackle ANY type of development, not just one particular type.

The development process

So, what exactly does the small-scale property development journey involve?

At a high level, the process is straightforward and reasonably logical:

1. *Finding the deal*: First things first; no development can take place until you find a project

2. *Analysing the deal*: Each potential deal needs to be scrutinised to see if it stacks up. As we've already mentioned, the developer will be looking for a 20%+ profit on GDV, so we need to do our calculations to check that we can achieve this

3. *Negotiating the deal*: Working with the agent or vendor to agree on a price

4. *Appointing the professional team*: These are the people such as the architect, planning consultant, project manager, contractor, etc., that will be doing most of the heavy lifting on the project. Experienced developers will have this team in place already; however, new developers will need to build one

5. *Arranging the finance*: Sourcing the funding needed for the project from commercial lenders and private investors

6. *Securing the deal*: Once the funding is agreed, the purchase can go through

7. *Building out the project*: Several key stages will take place on-site, culminating in the completion of the build phase of the project

8. *Selling the units*: The final piece of the jigsaw is finding buyers for your development (or renting the units out, if you're keeping them)

While that may be the overall process, the developer is not involved to the same degree throughout. Typically, they'll be taking more of a back seat once the project starts on site since the scheme's project manager oversees progress on their behalf. The developer can expect to be more hands-on during the early stages. Their key responsibilities are finding and analysing deals, appointing their professional team, arranging finance, and completing the purchase. They'll then come back to the fore when the units are ready to be sold, liaising with the selling agent to get sales through as quickly as possible while achieving the best possible price.

The importance of leverage

Most homeowners and buy-to-let landlords are already familiar with the financial leverage that goes hand in hand with property ownership. Let's say you put down a 25% deposit on a property, with the bank giving you a mortgage for the remainder. When your property's value increases, you don't just get 25% of the upside; you get all of it. We'll be studying this in more detail later since it's critical to what makes property investment such a powerful strategy.

However, with property development, you're able to get much greater financial leverage than you can with buy-to-let investing. That's because instead of simply waiting for house prices to increase over time, you're using other people's money to force value into a property or piece of land by developing it over a much shorter timeframe. So, you'll not only get a much bigger uplift on the money you're borrowing, but you'll also benefit from this uplift far sooner.

But leverage for developers doesn't stop there. Arguably the most significant leveraged resource that developers have is their professional team. These are the people that physically deliver the developer's projects, and this amazing resource is out there, simply waiting to be tapped into.

An architect must study for many years to become qualified before working in an architectural practice to refine their craft. As a developer, you can hire that architect to work on your project for a relatively modest fee. Consequently, you instantly get all the benefits of that training, knowledge, and experience without having to learn any of the architect's technical skills yourself. The same basic premise is true of every one of the skills and disciplines you will need to bring in to develop your project.

You might be thinking this sounds a tad inequitable. After all, your professionals have studied hard and worked diligently to build their careers over many years. And then you come along with your fancy development project and take the lion's share of the spoils.

The reality, of course, is that you're being paid a premium because you're not technically 'being paid'. The architect still gets paid a fee even if you've built a complete horror show of a project that no one in their right mind wants to live in. The same goes for your other professionals; they all get paid irrespective of whether your project makes a profit. You're the only person taking any risk here, and that's because you're taking your income as profit rather than a fee. And while it's a riskier proposition, the upside is a lot greater as a result.

This resource leverage is one of the big attractions of property development. Most of the skills you need are readily available to hire without learning how to do them yourself. And it's not as if these professionals are difficult to find, nor do you need to convince them to work for you. Being paid a fee by a developer to work on a project is what they do, day in day out. We'll be talking in more detail about the skills you need to have as a developer later on, but hopefully, you can see why development is one of the most highly leveraged business models there is. Developers use other people's money, expertise, and labour to create profit for themselves. And while the developer takes most of the financial reward, their entrepreneurship has also created wealth for the lenders and professional team members along the way while also creating new homes for people to live in.

Who is property development good for?

By the end of this book, we hope you'll appreciate that small-scale property development is a strategy that can be tackled successfully by a broad range of people. There are so many options regarding the scale and type of development you can take on.

So, who might become a property developer?

Newbies

We're talking here about people who are not yet involved in the world of property. They might own their own home, but they don't have rental properties, they've never done a flip, and certainly haven't tried their hand at development. Nor are they someone who works in the industry, such as an architect, or structural engineer. Basically, they are new to property investing, full stop.

You might be thinking that, as a newbie, you'd be at a massive disadvantage due to your lack of property experience. However, there are a couple of reasons why development is a good fit for you:

1. In development, you're leveraging the expertise of other people while using your existing skills. This is hugely powerful; there can't be too many other industries where you can create a six-figure income working in your spare time with no prior industry knowledge or experience. What ARE important are the key skills that you DO bring to the table, namely people skills, organisational skills, management skills, and decision-making skills
2. You will be using other people's money to develop property; you don't need to have any investment capital of your own (although having a small amount will make your journey easier)

Business Owners

Business owners have a massive advantage when it comes to development, even if their current day job has nothing to do with property. They typically already have the essential organisational, management, people, and decision-making skills that developers require; in fact, these are the same skills that every entrepreneur needs. Unlike employees, if business owners aren't proactive, their business will fail, so they already have exactly the right type of entrepreneurial mindset and tenacity that are required for development.

Business owners also tend to have more flexibility than people in a day job, which is key to be able to set aside enough time not only to get things off the ground but also to be able to deal with urgent issues as and when they arise.

Landlords

In many respects, landlords are the perfect candidates for small-scale property development, and many already develop their own projects.

Landlords typically have more property knowledge than newbies (even though it may not relate to development specifically). They often have more experience of sourcing (and using) property professionals, so it's easier for them to establish a professional team. But most landlords run out of cash to buy new rental properties, so their portfolios stall. To buy the next property they need another deposit, and that's where a development strategy can help in a big way.

Development sits at the 'opposite' end of the property spectrum to renting, and so landlords will be taking advantage of two contrasting yet complementary strategies. With income arriving from both their rental portfolio and their development projects, they end up having two streams of income instead of one, allowing them to both diversify their business and grow their portfolios much more quickly.

Professionals and Other Property Strategists

Here we would include people who work in the development or construction industry such as estate agents, architects, planning consultants, brokers, lenders, contractors, and the like. These people have a good understanding of the world of development; however, they may only have witnessed it from one perspective. Many will have compared their fees from a project with the profits made by the developer and thought it was about time they swapped places ☺.

The term 'other property strategists' includes people who make money from property without owning the underlying asset, such as rent-to-rent and serviced accommodation specialists.

All these people are well placed to get into development as they'll have good connections in the industry and a reasonable understanding of the world of property, even if it's specific to one strategy or discipline.

Who is property development not so good for?

Luckily, it's a relatively short list, and it relates more to people's general skillsets and their character traits, rather than the job they currently do:

1. People who do not have good people, management, organisational and decision-making skills
2. People who lack humility or who find it difficult to take advice
3. People who are very risk averse

4. People who don't like hard work, are not open-minded and are unwilling to learn
5. People who can't operate outside their comfort zones
6. People who aren't action-takers
7. People who aren't tenacious and persistent
8. People who lack any flexibility in their day job to be able to make occasional calls or meetings
9. People looking for a get rich quick solution

So, we've told you that property development can be lucrative and lots of people have the skills to do it. So why isn't everyone in the entire country a property developer?

There are several reasons:

They don't teach this stuff in school

Anyone who's read Rich Dad, Poor Dad and other similar books will appreciate that there's quite a lot of personal finance knowledge that we <u>don't</u> teach in schools. Instead, the model we teach people is to go and get the best qualifications you can so you can get a decent nine-to-five job which you can then work in until you retire albeit with the occasional promotion thrown in. We don't teach people that they can earn six-figures working part time leveraging other people's expertise and using other people's money. This is a good thing, because we don't want every kid leaving school wanting to become a property developer, however it goes some way to explaining why people don't automatically consider property development as an investment strategy.

It sounds complicated and risky

If you had to build a project yourself, it would be horrendously complicated, and to be honest, we probably wouldn't want to live in it – no offence ☺. Luckily, you won't be laying a single brick. There <u>is</u> risk involved, however we'll be talking later about how we mitigate the risk on every project. Ultimately profit is a risk vs reward business; the important part is how you manage the risk and avoid losing any money.

People think you need a lot of money to do it

You do, but people wrongly assume it has to be their own money, or that no one would lend them any of theirs. We'll be looking at this in detail, but the reality is you need relatively little of your own cash to develop property.

The name puts people off

People think of the term 'property developer' and it sounds like a career or job title. Some will think 'how could you be a property developer and have another job?'. People also often think that property developers only do larger projects, building housing estates worth millions. The reality is that development can start very much smaller, as we shall see. And it's certainly something that can be done in your spare time.

Introducing the 8 Pillars

We mentioned that over the last four decades, Ritchie had developed a system for developing property. We call it the 8 Pillars, and it's designed to make life a lot easier for developers, as they follow a logical series of steps rather than adopting a more ad hoc approach. It also ensures that the fundamental building blocks of a successful development business are put in place from the outset on every project.

Now, we've already promised that this isn't going to be a how-to manual for development. However, we thought it only fair to give you a brief overview of what's covered in each of these 8 Pillars so that you can understand how we break things down. That pleasure awaits you in the final part of the book.

So, in this chapter, we've covered a few of the fundamental principles involved in development. We now want to give you a sense of what impact small-scale property development can have when you do it properly. After all, the whole point of doing it is to make a profit, but exactly what sort of profits are achievable? We also wanted to compare the results you can get from development with those of a buy-to-let strategy, as we know many people may be weighing up both options or they may be existing landlords who are thinking about getting into development.

Now, we could have put together lots of diagrams with natty numbers and footnotes, showing exactly how things stacked up. But we felt that wouldn't bring things to life or do it justice.

So, instead, we thought we'd tell you a story.

3. The Property Investor's Tale

In our experience, stories are often the best way of illustrating and explaining things, and hopefully, this will prove to be no exception. Cards on the table, we're going to let the story play out at a high level since if we throw in all the detail, it could be a little distracting. But if you catch yourself thinking that we've over-simplified things a bit, don't worry; we'll be filling in any important details afterward. It's the principle that's important at this point; we want you to appreciate the art of the possible.

And we should warn you that there are a few numbers involved. You won't need a maths degree to understand them, but it's worth pausing when you get to them to make sure they've sunk in. After all, it's the numbers that will make you the profit.

So, without any further ado, let's jump in...

Tom's Story

Once upon a time, two work colleagues, Tom and Vicki, decided they wanted to change their lives. They'd usually meet up in the Red Lion every Friday after work and would often reflect on their rather humdrum existence working for their mutual employer, Kismet Financial. Just two middle managers working the 9 to 5 (which was usually more like 8 to 6), wondering if there shouldn't be a little bit more to life, and speculating on what exactly the future might have in store for them.

Now, if this sounds a little bit depressing, don't worry. They certainly weren't unhappy. Things were ok. They each had nice homes and a young family, with partners who loved them. They could afford to go on holiday each year. They also had hobbies; Tom played the guitar, and Vicki wrote short stories. So, while life wasn't a complete bowl of cherries every single day, it certainly wasn't terrible by any means. A bit like most people, perhaps.

And just like most people, they also had their dreams and aspirations. Tom was very clear about what he wanted. A five-bedroomed house in one of the local villages, with a new Range Rover on the drive, and the money to take his wife, Sandra, and their two kids on nice holidays every year. As for Vicki, she wanted a private education for her daughter and to be able to afford for her husband, David, to quit the travelling sales job he hated because it kept him away from his family. Nothing earth-shattering for either of them. No super-yachts or country estates. Just a nicer life. And they always enjoyed sharing and refining their respective wish lists with each other, although Tom still couldn't believe Vicki didn't have a Range Rover on hers. What was wrong with the woman?

And so each Friday at 6pm, they would both reflect on the ups and downs of their week, and inevitably the conversation would turn to the future. What lay in store for them at Kismet Financial? Maybe a promotion at some point, with a pay rise to go with it? That would be nice, but it wouldn't exactly be life-changing. The bigger house, the nicer car, and fancier holidays were not something Tom could see himself living in, driving in, or going on, anytime soon. Not unless some ageing boy band heard him playing the guitar and signed him up on the spot, which he thought sounded rather unlikely. And, if she were honest, Vicki was pretty much resigned to her daughter's state education and her husband's perennial absences, at least for the foreseeable future.

Ever the pragmatist, Vicki also knew that success wasn't just about having the finer things in life right now or even in the next few years. It was their long-term future that was the most important thing. She had sat down and worked out what her and David's finances would look like when they retired, and there was no way of dressing it up; things weren't looking pretty. Everything feels fine when there's a salary or two coming in, but as soon as you retire, the money dries up, yet the expenses don't. At that point, it's all about whatever nest egg or pension you've been able to stash away during your career. And while David had been a little dismissive ('don't worry, I'm sure we'll be ok. After all, it's not as if we're retiring any time soon!'), Vicki wondered whether they'd ever be able to retire at all. It was all very well thinking that a silver bullet would come along at some point and change things. But she worried that this was precisely what everyone else thought, right up to the point when they discovered they needed to get a supermarket job in their seventies to make ends meet. After all, how many people ever bothered to project what their income will be later in life?

As it turned out, it was Vicki's comment about working in a supermarket that had caused Tom to pause mid-pint one Friday evening and stare thoughtfully across his glass at her as the early evening crowd filed noisily into the pub. She could see his cogs whirring, but it wasn't until the following Monday that it became clear what had been going through his mind. He'd caught up with her in the office canteen and told her excitedly he'd spent the weekend working out his own retirement numbers, and the penny had dropped big time. It was, he announced rather grandly, high time they stopped talking about their dreams and started doing something about making them a reality. Was she in? Vicki looked at her plate thoughtfully for a moment and twirled the remnants of an anaemic-looking sausage on her fork. Then she looked at Tom's earnest face and smiled. You bet she was.

The following month or so went by in a blur. Each week, they would spend their spare time poring over books, magazines, and the internet trying to find the best strategy for changing their fortunes, then meet up at the Red Lion on Friday to compare notes. There were so many options. The stock market was the early front-runner, but it soon became apparent that to make decent returns as a stock picker, you either had to be very lucky or spend a lot of time researching the market. Neither of them could afford to leave their jobs, so whatever strategy they adopted would have to fit into their spare time.

Tom had previously signed up for a fantasy stock trading account where he could invest imaginary dollars on the stock market to test exactly how easy it was. He was amazed that even his most logical of stock purchases could suddenly lose half their value on a whiff of sentiment, while some of his other stocks would increase for no apparent reason, as far as he could tell. Of course, you could avoid the peaks and troughs by buying a tracker fund of some description or sticking to the blue chips, but the returns didn't look very exciting. In some years, the funds had even moved backward, so he reluctantly decided that the stock market wasn't going to be the best solution.

After many weeks of going around the houses on many different money-making ideas, the strategy they kept coming back to was the property market. After all, it was a tried and tested model. They'd discovered that property prices had doubled on average every ten years or so, and unlike stocks and shares, property is a tangible asset that can't lose all its value overnight. Better still, it goes up in value without you having to do very much other than wait. And, of course, you could rent it out while you waited, which gave you income as well as equity growth. So, having settled on property as a strategy, they agreed to put together their own individual ten-year road map, and the following Friday, they met at the Red Lion to share their respective plans.

At the allotted hour, Vicki got the drinks in and insisted that Tom reveal his strategy first, which he did, excitedly showing her the projections on his spreadsheet. When he'd finished, she smiled and congratulated him. His plan was straightforward and would undoubtedly go a long way towards achieving a more secure financial future, although she told him it might take him more than ten years to get to where he really wanted. Tom's new Range Rover might need to wait a bit longer, she'd joked.

When it was time to reveal her own plan, she suddenly felt uneasy. What had seemed quite logical at home on her kitchen table now sounded risky and complicated compared to Tom's very simple strategy. Still, beggars can't be choosers, she told herself. She opened her computer and walked Tom through her idea. When she'd finished, Tom gave her a thoughtful look. It would be a great plan if it worked, but did she really think she could pull it off? And it sounded pretty complicated… Was she sure about the numbers, as they looked a bit… well, aggressive? She told him she'd done her research and had confidence that her plan, while a little off-piste, would deliver results. She just had to commit to it.

She hoped she sounded more confident than she felt…

The next day, Tom started to put his plan into action. His strategy was very simple; he would find a buy-to-let property and then rent it out. This was about as vanilla a strategy as you could get, and he was confident he could sort everything out in his spare time. He was nowhere near as convinced about Vicki's plan, which frankly sounded like a lot of work, but he knew she didn't have as much capital to invest as he did. But he was very determined for his own plan to succeed.

Luckily for Tom, he had been able to pull together quite a chunky deposit. He and Sandra had some savings, plus he was shortly due a bonus from work. But it was a rather unexpected cash gift from his parents that had made the biggest difference. He now had the princely sum of £60k, which he could use to buy his first buy-to-let property. He'd allowed £10k for stamp duty and other fees, which left him £50k as a deposit. Having researched the best area and best property type to buy, he went and bought a three-bed house for £200k, having first secured a 75% buy-to-let mortgage from his bank.

Stage 1 of the plan now complete, Tom and Sandra went straight on to stage 2. This involved giving the property a bit of a makeover to ensure it would rent easily and get a good yield. Several dozen tins of paint and a lot of elbow grease later, Tom found himself showing an impressed letting agent around the property, feeling decidedly pleased with himself. And sure enough, within a week, the agent had secured some tenants; a young couple called the Joneses who had recently got married and who both worked locally. They would be paying £1,000 per month in rent, and this would cover the £400 monthly mortgage repayment, plus the £200 of other costs such as the agent's fees, the insurances, and running repairs. Which left Tom and Sandra a tidy £400 profit at the end of every month. So far, their plan was coming along nicely.

Tom's First Project

Property purchased for: £200k (of which £150k was borrowed on a buy-to-let mortgage and £50k deposit was put in by Tom)

Purchase costs: £10k (funded by Tom)

Rental Income: £1,000 per month

Bills: £600 per month

Profit: £400 per month or £4,800 per year

We now need to roll the clock forward quite a bit, ten years to be precise. And it turns out that quite a lot of water has passed under the bridge. Somewhat unexpectedly, Tom and Sandra had had another baby (their third), which meant they needed to boost their income. Luckily, Tom had been able to find a job working in another city which paid much better than his role at Kismet Financial. After much consideration, the family had decided to up sticks and make the move. Tom was pleased to have upgraded his car, although it wasn't yet the Range Rover that still adorned his wish list. And their house was marginally bigger than their old one, although they managed to fill it up with so much stuff that it somehow seemed smaller. But everyone was healthy and reasonably happy.

Tom's only real regret ten years on was that he'd lost contact with Vicki. She'd left Kismet shortly after he had, and she'd called Tom to give him her new phone number and email address. He'd written it down on a piece of paper and carefully put it in his shirt pocket, promising he'd be in touch soon. Later that evening, he'd rather less carefully tossed the shirt in the washing basket, and the washing machine had predictability done what washing machines do. He'd promised himself he'd do some digging on the internet to track her down, but somehow the months and then the years had rolled by, and he'd never got round to it. Every so often, she would flit into his thoughts. He'd been fond of Vicki, and he hoped everything had turned out well for her.

This morning Tom was in a particularly good mood as he was about to start stage 3 of his ten-year plan, which was to buy his second buy-to-let property. His ten-year plan had become a twenty-year plan once he'd realised he needed to keep going for a while longer to achieve the numbers he was looking for. He'd smiled to himself when he'd remembered Vicki telling him that's exactly what he'd need to do all those years ago.

Tom had also saved up the monthly rental profits from the Joneses (who were succeeded by the Khans, then the Robinsons). His £400 monthly profit had kept pace with inflation and was now nudging

£515 a month. Their total rental profit over the ten years had been £60k, which meant he could now afford to put down a £50k deposit on another £200k house, allowing for £10k in fees.

There was some more good news too. Tom and Sandra's first £200k house had doubled in value since he bought it, and it was now worth £400k. It meant that while they still had a buy-to-let mortgage of £150k, their equity had grown from £50k to £250k simply by waiting ten years. And of course, the £50k in rental profit they'd made over that time was the reason they could now afford to buy house number two. Overall, they'd managed to turn their initial £50k investment into £300k in just ten years.

Tom and Sandra had carefully thought through their next steps, as they knew they had a choice to make. By buying a second property, they would now have doubled their rental profit each month, which over the next ten years would amount to some £120k. Also, during the same period, the first house should double in value again to £800k, and the second house would double in value to £400k. In another ten years' time, this would leave them with £300k in mortgages, total equity of £900k, and rental profits of £130k. It meant they would have managed to turn their initial £50k investment into over £1m within twenty years, which wasn't bad going.

But it was Sandra who'd raised a good point, and it had really got Tom thinking. She'd noticed that most of their profit came from the financial leverage they were getting from the bank. If they had initially bought a £50k property outright, it would have doubled in value over ten years to £100k. But by purchasing a £200k property using a mortgage, they'd turned that same £50k investment into £250k. So, she asked, was there a way they could use some of the equity they'd built up in their first property to buy even more houses?

Tom had gone to his mortgage advisor, and together they'd hatched a plan. They should be able to remortgage their first buy-to-let property (that was now worth £400k) to free up some cash. It would mean getting a new mortgage for £200k and then paying back the original £150k they'd borrowed, leaving them £50k as a deposit for a third house.

Tom's Phase 2 property purchases after 10 years

Property #1 bought for: £200k (£150k mortgage plus a £50k deposit) ten years ago

Current value of Property #1: £400k (Tom's total equity now £250k)

Remortgaged Property #1:   Tom remortgaged Property #1 (now worth £400k) by taking out a new mortgage of £200k and using it to repay the original £150k buy-to-let mortgage. The £50k balance along with the rental profits from Property #1 was used to purchase two more properties (Properties #2 & #3), and following the remortgage, he now had equity of £200k in Property #1

Property #2 & #3 bought for: £200k each, of which £150k was borrowed on a buy-to-let mortgage and £50k deposit was put in by Tom, with £10k purchase costs funded by Tom)

Rental Profit: £1,315 per month or £15,780 per year (£515 for Property #1 and £400 for #2 and #3)

Tom reworked his numbers considering this new approach and ran through them with Sandra, who was clearly establishing herself as the strategic brains of the operation. In another ten years' time, the first house would have doubled in value again, to £800k, giving them £600k in equity once the new £200k remortgage was accounted for. And the two new houses would have doubled to £400k apiece, with equity between them of £500k, bringing Tom and Sandra's total equity to £1.1m. Tom reckoned their rental profits over the next ten years from the three houses would total £200k, as they had increased the rent to account for the increased cost of their remortgage repayments.

Overall, they would have turned their original £60k investment into £1.3m in 20 years, some 30% better than their original stage 3 plan. And so, that's exactly what they decided to do.

We now need to do a bit more time travelling, you've guessed it, by leaping forward another ten years. This time, we find Tom driving through the late December traffic on a wintery Friday afternoon. It's dark, and the city is bright and busy, with people out and about doing their last-minute Christmas shopping. There's a smattering of snow in the air that flicks across Tom's windscreen, and it seems to be getting heavier. Could they be in a for a white Christmas? It was certainly looking possible. At least the kids would be pleased, he thought.

At that moment, Tom's car passed by the empty Kismet Financial building, which now cut a rather forlorn figure on the city's outskirts. It had stood empty for quite a while. He'd heard it was due to be converted into apartments by some enterprising developer. How fortunes can change, thought Tom. Who'd have predicted that his old employer would become yet another casualty of the recession? He was relieved he no longer worked there, although given nearly twenty years had passed since he had, it seemed like a different life. Yet he liked to keep up to speed with events in this part of the world, even though he'd long since moved away. After all, his three buy-to-let properties were a mile down the road, and he felt obliged to check up on them occasionally.

The traffic was getting worse, and ahead of him, he could make out the familiar glow of the Red Lion in the distance. The estate agent's office he was visiting lay just ahead, but there were no free parking spaces outside the building. He'd no sooner resigned himself to trying the multi-storey around the corner when a car suddenly pulled out of a space right in front of him. He quickly dived into it, waved a hasty apology to the vehicle behind, and pulled up tight behind a dark blue late-model Range Rover parked at the side of the road. Very smart, he thought, his eyes enviously taking in the gleaming coachwork. He could do with something like that, particularly if it kept snowing at this rate. He stepped out into the street and, turning his collar against the icy breeze, headed briskly across the pavement.

As he opened the door, he was greeted by a welcome blast of warm air, which had also done a great job of steaming up the estate agency's windows. Not that there would be many people window-shopping in this weather, he thought. He introduced himself to the receptionist who ushered him to a nearby desk and went off to find Simon, the senior negotiator that Tom was due to meet.

As he waited, he reflected on how his plan had turned out. Twenty years on, and he felt he was doing ok. Slow and steady wins the race, or so they say. The numbers that he and Sandra had projected had more or less materialised, and here he was, looking to buy three more houses to add to their portfolio. It would mean that he'd be able to retire in a few years. They would be getting quite a healthy rental profit from their six units, plus their equity was increasing every year. If they needed some cash, they could always remortgage one of the houses. When you added in their savings and Tom's work pension, it looked like they would be quite comfortably off. It might soon be time to start thinking about that Range Rover, after all. That is, assuming Sandra was willing to let him have one.

Just then, the branch manager's door at the rear of the office opened, and Simon appeared, hurrying towards Tom across the shop floor. He shook Tom warmly by the hand and apologised for keeping him waiting, telling him a big client had just been signed up and that his boss had wanted Simon to meet them. But he'd managed to extricate himself, and boy, did he have some excellent properties to show Tom. He opened a manilla folder, pulled out a sheaf of particulars, and began to run through them with the enthusiasm reserved exclusively for the estate agents of this world.

Tom's Phase 3 property purchases after 20 years	
Property #1 bought for:	£200k (£150k mortgage plus a £50k deposit) twenty years ago then remortgaged for £200k ten years ago
Current value of Property #1:	£800k (Tom's total equity now £600k)
Current value of Property #2:	£400k (Tom's total equity £250k)
Current value of Property #3:	£400k (Tom's total equity £250k)
Total Equity:	£1.1m
Total Rental Profit:	£200k over last 20 years
Net Profit:	£1.3m
Annual Rental Profit:	£16k

Ten minutes later, Tom had put his name down for a couple of viewings. One looked particularly hopeful as it was on the same street as his first property, and the price looked sensible. He might even be able to negotiate a discount if he played his cards right. He gathered up the particulars and thanked Simon for his time. As he rose from his seat, the manager's office door opened again, and a man and a woman emerged. Tom checked his watch. Almost closing time. Probably the office staff wanting to get home quickly before the snow set in. He certainly couldn't blame them.

As he shook Simon's hand, his attention was drawn to one of the emerging figures, a slim, elegant woman in a fine cashmere coat. Something looked familiar about her, but he couldn't put his finger on it. She had her back to him and was talking to someone seated at one of the far desks, presumably saying goodbye to a colleague. As he headed towards the door, he saw her start to move towards the exit too. It looked like this was his chance to do a good deed for the day, holding the door open for a lady. Sandra would be impressed, he thought, smiling to himself.

He grabbed the brass handle and swung the big glass door open, turning towards the approaching figure as he did so. And his gaze widened in surprise as he instantly recognised a face he'd not set eyes on in almost twenty years.

4. The Property Developer's Tale

Vicki's story

Life, as it turns out, is full of surprises, thought Vicki. On a day when to be fair, she had expected to have a few flashbacks, here she was having a full-on Groundhog Day experience. Sitting in the Red Lion at 6pm on a Friday chewing the cud with Tom once more. Admittedly a more distinguished-looking and perhaps slightly portlier Tom. But it was unmistakeably Tom, nonetheless. Who'd have thought that after so much time had passed, they'd meet unexpectedly just a stone's throw away from their old haunts? And in an estate agent's, of all places.

Having oscillated randomly between, 'I can't believe it!', 'You look amazing!', and 'I'm so sorry not to have been in touch', Tom seemed to have calmed down now they were safely ensconced in their familiar spot. She looked around the place. It was pretty much as she'd remembered it from twenty years ago. There may have been a lick of paint applied at some point, and she was pretty sure the carpet was a different shade. But otherwise, it was the same old Red Lion. Even the menu looked the same, not that she'd ever been tempted to indulge.

And after five minutes chatting to Tom, she remembered why she had warmed to him when they'd first met at Kismet Financial. Good old Tom, you really haven't changed much, she thought. Although she wasn't entirely sure the same could be said about her.

For the first twenty minutes, they reminisced about the old days, and then Tom couldn't wait to bring her up to speed on how his ten-year plan had worked out. And how, much to Vicki's amusement, it had turned into a twenty-year plan. Tom reluctantly agreed it was probably going to be a thirty-year plan, given that he was now buying more property and still didn't have that Range Rover. But Vicki was genuinely thrilled that it all seemed to be working out for him.

And then came the obvious question. How had things worked out for Vicki, given her modest budget and slightly off-piste strategy? Tom was feeling anxious about learning the answer, given he'd just been shooting his mouth off about his own success. He'd feel dreadful if it had all gone to pot for her. And he presumed that, since she now appeared to be working for an estate agent, things might not have gone totally to plan. Vicki had a long pull on her drink and took a deep breath. Here goes, she thought. Let's see what you make of this.

Her original problem had been a lack of funds. She and David had just about been able to scrape £10,000 together between them, but that was pretty much everything they'd had. It would be a sizeable deposit on a car, but it wasn't anything like enough for a deposit on a buy-to-let property. There simply weren't any properties for sale at such a low price. Which meant she had had to come up with a different approach, and her research had led her in a different direction to the usual buy-to-let or rent-to-rent strategies. Steve, an old school friend of David's who owned a couple of hair salons, had done several small property developments and was waxing lyrical in the pub one evening about how it was a lot more straightforward than most people thought. He hadn't even needed to get planning permission. He simply converted a shop into flats, and when he needed more cash, he'd do another one. But as far as Vicki was concerned, she really couldn't see how developing a property could be described as straightforward, particularly if you'd never done it before.

Yet there was something that Steve had said which had seriously piqued her interest. He'd mentioned that he'd invested just £10k of his own money in his last project. This, she felt, merited further investigation. So, later that evening, Vicki suggested to David that he invite Steve and his lovely girlfriend Natasha over for dinner sometime very soon. David was a little surprised, given that Steve and Natasha hadn't previously been anywhere close to appearing on Vicki's rather exclusive dinner invitee list. Nor to his knowledge had the adjective 'lovely' ever been routinely used to describe Natasha, least of all by his wife. But he knew better than to ask, and a date was duly put in the diary for the following week.

On the appointed evening, things went more or less according to plan. Vicki's mushroom linguine had, as usual, been a riotous success. Several bottles of Stella had loosened Steve's tongue nicely, and much to his surprise, David had, at Vicki's firm direction, expressed an interest in acquiring a Bichon Frise. This sent Natasha into raptures, and she and David sloped off to the kitchen where she could give him chapter and verse on her favourite subject. This left Steve in the lounge, gushing nicely about his developments to a sober and very inquisitive Vicki, notebook in hand.

Once their dinner guests had poured themselves into a cab at the end of the evening, Vicki took stock. One slightly bemused husband, an empty case of Stella, and a dozen pages of notes on the minutiae of Steve's development projects. All told, the evening had gone pretty well, she thought. All she needed to do now was formulate a plan.

The key to it all, she felt, was understanding how the numbers worked. Steve had said he'd bought his last project, a disused shop, for £300k and had borrowed 70% of the cost from a commercial lender who specialised in property development. This meant Steve needed to find the remaining £90k deposit himself, which Vicki thought sounded odd given he'd mentioned he'd only invested £10k of his own money. But with the commercial lender's blessing, Steve had lined up some private investors who had agreed to lend him 100% of his deposit. And these investors were quite happy because Steve was paying them interest at 10% per annum, which he'd pointed out was a heck of a lot more than they could get from anywhere else.

Vicki suddenly had a thought. Surely there were some costs involved in buying the property that sat outside the £90k deposit. Who paid for those? Good question, said Steve, relishing his captive audience, and feeling he'd dodged a bullet on the Bichon Frise front. He'd told her he always expected to pay a few thousand in additional fees relating to the purchase. Firstly, there were his solicitor's costs and the cost of the survey. Then there was the stamp duty to pay, plus some architect's fees and planning consultant fees related to some work they did pre-purchase. It amounted to about £10k in total, he'd said, although he added that he could simply have upped the amount of money he'd borrowed from private investors to cover it, had he wanted to.

So far, so good. But how could he develop the flats if he didn't have any more cash left? That's simple, said Steve; the same commercial lender that lent him the 70% to buy the shop also lent him 100% of the development finance as well. He didn't get it all upfront; it was released to his contractor in stages as the project progressed. But Steve didn't have to fund any of the development costs himself. Much to Vicki's surprise, it turned out that commercial lenders funding 100% of the development costs was standard practice.

Vicki had then asked him how much the development costs were, and he'd replied that they had come in at around £350k. She didn't know whether that was expensive or not, but it still amounted to a large sum of money. And what's more, Steve said, he didn't need to pay a single penny back to either the commercial lender or his private investors until the flats were sold and his money was in his bank account. How cool was that?

This was proving to be quite an education, and Vicki was scribbling away furiously. She knew that with a buy-to-let mortgage, you start paying interest immediately. So, to have a deal where you only paid back the interest after you'd made your profit seemed like a big win, particularly if you didn't have lots of spare cash.

She mentioned this to Steve, who laughed and told her that, no, this wasn't the best part. The best part was that the commercial lender had allowed him to be paid a development management fee of £30k during the project's construction phase. What about that!

At this point, Vicki was beginning to regret having plied the man with quite so much alcohol. She was finding it a little difficult to understand all the figures he was firing at her. But after a bit more probing, she'd been able to establish that, as the developer, Steve had been able to take a fee from the project for his role in heading it all up. Understandably, lenders want to make sure a development doesn't stall because the developer is struggling financially. So, they let Steve be paid a management fee during the development phase (effectively advance profit), so he remained focused on getting the project across the line. And, of course, the fees for everyone else working on the project were also paid by the development finance.

This was sounding better and better, thought Vicki. But the next few questions would be critical. What did he sell the flats for, how long did the project take, and what profit did he make overall? Her pen hovered expectantly over her notebook.

By now, there was no holding Steve back. He'd said he'd sold the flats for a total of £850k, and the project had taken 18 months from start to finish. With the shop and the development costs coming in at £650k combined, it meant he'd pocketed a profit of £200k, give or take. In fact, the commercial lender had insisted that Steve target at least a 20% profit against the £850k selling price, but he'd managed to make a bit more than that.

Steve's Project

Shop bought for: £300k (of which £210k borrowed from a commercial lender and £90k from private investors)

Purchase costs: £10k (funded by Steve)

Development Costs: £350k (100% funded by the commercial lender)

GDV: £850k (what the flats were sold for)

Net Profit: £190k (including £30k Development Management Fee that Steve was paid during the project)

Timescale: 18 months

Vicki was amazed. Steve had taken just 18 months to turn £10k into almost £200k working in his spare time. He'd paid back his private investors as well as the commercial lender and settled every bill from his professional team. He'd even managed to earn £30k from the project before he'd finished building it! The project was completed with nothing left to do, and he'd made a profit that was over six times the national average wage.

Vicki's next question was an obvious one. Exactly how difficult was it to run a development project. This, she figured, would be her biggest hurdle since she really didn't have a clue where to start. Then again, Steve hadn't immediately struck her as property developer material, although he evidently already had several projects under his belt. And Steve's response had genuinely surprised her.

He'd told her that it took a fair bit of effort to start with, but none of it was difficult; just time-consuming, as finding the right deal took time and effort, as did learning how the development process worked. But in essence, all he'd done was found a building to convert, worked with a cost consultant to understand if it would make a 20% profit, asked a broker to go and find him a commercial lender who would lend him the money, and found some private investors who were happy to receive a 10% return. He'd then found a team of professionals to do the work, but to be honest, his Project Manager had recommended most of them. Finally, he'd appointed an estate agent to sell the finished apartments.

Ok, please could he rewind a moment, she'd asked, scribbling furiously. What was all this about a Project Manager? Was Steve saying that he hadn't managed the project himself? Absolutely right, he'd replied. The last thing he wanted to be was a project manager, far too much like hard work! But because the construction budget ran to a healthy six figures, the project could afford to appoint a professional Project Manager to oversee everything. The PM would go to the site and supervise the contractor, the design team, and everyone else, and Steve just had a weekly phone call with him to find out how things were going. He'd been asked to make a few decisions occasionally by the PM, but that was about it. And once the flats were finished, Steve had appointed an estate agent to sell them, which was all very straightforward. He'd spent quite a lot of time at the start finding the property, selecting a team, and getting the finance sorted. But once the work started, he reckoned he only spent about an hour a week working on it.

This was all sounding too good to be true. Vicki had had visions of her having to go on-site as a complete newbie surrounded by all these highly experienced professionals, feeling entirely out of her depth. But it turns out that this is what her Project Manager would do on her behalf, which came as a massive relief.

However, Vicki wasn't about to set up a property development business on the strength of a half-cut salon owner's tipsy ramblings, so she made a point of asking Steve for his list of contacts. And over the next week and a half, she managed to meet with most of them, the architect, the contractor, the project manager, and several others. They'd all verified what Steve had said, plus she'd gleaned lots of other very interesting information to boot. More than ever, she was convinced that this was the strategy she should be pursuing. She chatted it through with David, who gave his blessing provided he no longer had to feign a passion for pooches. Smiling, she reluctantly agreed, then immediately swung into action.

On Steve's advice, the first thing she did was create a name for her new development business. After a little pondering, she'd settled on 'Lorien Developments', which, apart from being her daughter's middle name, also happened to be the name of the 'God of Dreams'. Rather appropriate, she thought with a wry smile. She ordered some business cards, paid a modest sum for a local web designer to build her a simple website, and within two weeks, she had a brand.

The next item on her to-do list was to pull together a team. This had turned out to be a lot easier than she was expecting, which was a blessing since she could count the number of property development professionals she knew personally on no hands. Vicki knew she could have searched online to find the people she needed, but how would she know whether they were any good? In the end, she'd decided to go on recommendations. Vicki had started with Steve's project manager, Martin, as Steve had been highly complimentary about him. Then she'd simply asked Martin to recommend other professionals that would be a good fit for the sort of projects she was looking to do. Then, whenever she met one of these recommended people, Vicki would ask them to recommend other professionals in turn. Soon, she had a pretty good idea of who the movers and shakers were for all the major positions on her team. And of course, she didn't have to pay these people anything at this point; they were simply her first-choice appointees once she had a project for them to work on.

At Steve's suggestion, the other thing she did was to ask each team member she'd selected if it was ok to put their picture and a brief paragraph about them on her website, depicting them as one of Lorien Developments' preferred partners. Not only was this kudos for the professional, but it also meant that anyone looking at Vicki's website would see an array of talented and experienced people who were all part of Lorien's team. Wasn't this a little disingenuous, she'd asked Steve? After all, Lorien Developments hadn't yet developed anything other than a website. Steve had assured her that no one expected her to do the technical drawings, lay the bricks, or understand the planning rules, so it was much more appropriate that people could see the individuals and businesses who would be doing this work on Lorien's behalf. Plus, of course, it would give them a great deal of confidence that she had a great team behind her.

With her team in place, the next step was one she felt somewhat more anxious about; finding the money. She was very conscious that with only £10k to play with, she might not look a particularly attractive proposition, despite Steve's assurances. So it was with some trepidation that she'd walked into the office of Steve's commercial finance broker, Darren, to understand what he could do for her.

After she'd explained about her new business and the type and scale of the projects she was looking to build, Darren had asked her some questions about her own financial position. Half expecting him to wince when she told him about her modest means, she'd been pleasantly surprised by his reaction. He'd explained that he had several lenders that would be interested in working with Vicki and who would be happy for her to source her deposits from private investors. Having taken some more information, he said to leave it with him. He would speak to the lenders to get a decision in principle and would let her know in due course. She had left Darren's office with a small spring in her step, reflecting how great it was that her broker would be doing all the legwork to find her a lender rather than herself. But she knew that her financial battle was far from over. She now needed to find some very nice people who would be happy to lend her lots of their hard-earned money to fund her deposit.

As it turned out, this had been both easier and more difficult than she'd expected. It was initially difficult because she didn't like asking people for money. She felt rather needy and awkward and found herself blushing and generally on the back foot. In the end, she'd decided to call Steve again, to get some advice, as she'd recalled he'd managed to raise £90k of private finance for his own project. Steve had been delighted to help. He confessed that he'd had the same struggle initially until he'd realised that there weren't many other places where private investors could get a 10% return, and as a result, he held most of the cards. So instead of asking for money, he'd presented it to potential investors as a limited investment opportunity that was by invitation only. He would also make a point of interviewing potential investors before inviting them to come on board to reinforce this exclusivity. As a result, he'd had people asking if they could lend <u>him</u> money rather than him having to ask them! She'd had to admire Steve's approach, as it neatly turned who was buying and who was selling on its head. He'd also told her to think of everyone as a potential investor since you just never knew. Private investors don't wear a badge, he'd joked, so just make sure you tell everyone what you do.

The other piece of advice Steve gave her was to look close to home. He'd initially assumed that none of his friends or family would have any money to invest. But once he'd hinted that there was an investment opportunity, he'd been surprised to find several people come forward who were interested. People don't talk about their money, he'd said, but when they already know and trust you, you've got a massive head start. Eventually, he'd ended up getting most of his private investment from friends and family, and having been repaid once, people were delighted to keep on reinvesting.

Buoyed by Steve's advice, Vicki went to work. She asked her solicitor to email her a template loan agreement that she could share with potential investors. She also put together a small information pack that talked about Lorien Developments, the type of projects it was looking to do, and its professional team, including Vicki herself as its CEO. As she started speaking to people about Lorien, she quickly landed upon an 'elevator pitch' that seemed to work well. She discovered she could sense quite easily when the person she was talking to was interested in investing. If they were, she'd invite them out for a coffee (and, more often than not, a cake) where they could both talk about the opportunity in more detail and take things from there.

As it turned out, Steve had been right. She'd found several investors who she hadn't known personally, but they were friends of friends. Then much to her surprise, David's uncle had offered to invest a fair proportion of what she'd needed. They'd been at a family party, and Vicki had mentioned Lorien and slipped into her usual elevator pitch. It turned out that, as he was over fifty-five, he could take a tax-free lump sum from his pension. However, he'd not found anywhere to invest it until Vicki had mentioned Lorien. After several more conversations to discuss all the detail, he'd happily agreed to come on board.

In the end, she'd had £120k worth of private investment lined up from just six investors, and while she knew she might not need all of it, she also knew there was a risk that investors could drop out when the time came to ask them for the money. With Darren, the broker, having firmed up a decision in principle from a commercial lender and her private investors now in place, it was time to go and find a deal.

She quickly learned that this wasn't simply a question of popping onto an estate agent's website and choosing a project. As Steve had intimated, it took time, patience, imagination, research, and then a bit more patience. Some deals didn't stack up, while others got snapped up by people offering more money than she felt the building was worth. Intriguingly, it turned out that many deals were sold before they reached the open market, so she'd needed to forge good relationships with the commercial agents that covered her 'patch' to get a heads up when a decent opportunity was about to be taken on. She reckoned she must have looked at close to a hundred deals before she eventually heard about 5 Dillon Street.

The call came just as she was dropping off her daughter at school. It was from Anna, who worked at one of her local commercial agents and was someone with whom Vicki had made a point of striking up a good relationship. It hadn't taken long for Vicki to find out that they both had young daughters, and by staying in touch and occasionally taking Anna out for coffee at the local coffee shop in town, she'd built up a friendly albeit professional relationship with her. Sometimes Anna would give Vicki a heads up about properties that she was about to take on that might be of interest, and as it turned out, today was no exception.

Waiting for Anna outside 5 Dillon Street, she'd been struck by the ugliness of the building and by the beauty of its location. It was a bland, rather sad-looking light industrial unit that covered the entirety of the plot it sat on, little more than four walls and a roof, sitting on a concrete slab. But it was two minutes' walk to the train station, it was surrounded by houses and apartments, and it was in an area that estate agents referred to as 'up-and-coming'. And Vicki could readily visualise the six new flats she could build using permitted development rights. Plus, she knew that the numbers looked good if she could only get it for the right price, which was about £20k below what Anna had told her the owner wanted for it.

When Anna had finished showing her around, Vicki had suggested they retire to the small café tucked away in a courtyard off one of the side streets. As they sat down at one of the brightly coloured tables, Anna had told Vicki that the office had received an offer that morning for Dillon Street, which was very close to the asking price. But as Vicki's heart sank, Anna had smiled, and offered her a glimmer of hope. She hinted that the offer hadn't yet been accepted by the vendor since there was some doubt whether the prospective buyer could raise the required funds. Perhaps if Vicki's offer was a little closer to the asking price, it might tip the balance in her favour, given that Vicki had already ensured that her funding was in place. But her offer would have to come in sooner rather than later, Anna suggested.

As soon as she was back in the car, Vicki called her architect. Could he find a way to reduce the project's cost so that she could afford to increase her offer while still making the 20% profit that her commercial lender insisted on? After a nail-biting wait, he'd eventually called back. He reckoned he could shave around £20k from the overall costs by doing something rather clever with the floorplan, which shouldn't affect the selling price of the units. Her cost consultant had said she'd need to do some more detailed costings, but yes, a £20k saving sounded about right. And so Vicki made a call to Anna, feeling about as nervous and excited as she'd ever felt in her life, and made her increased offer. Could this finally be the one? Anna said she'd speak to her client and would get back to Vicki soon.

Later that afternoon, Vicki was waiting outside the school to collect her daughter along with a troupe of other mums and dads when the phone rang. She pulled it out of her pocket and looked at the screen. It was Anna. She took a deep breath, crossed her fingers, and answered it. A few moments later, her daughter ran towards her across the playground and was surprised to get a bigger than usual hug from her beaming and ever so slightly tearful mother. Vicki had just secured her first project.

What followed over the next few months was a steep learning curve, and it coincided with several other things that were going on in Vicki's life. David's employer had suddenly gone bust, which had come as a major shock to them both, but luckily, he had been able to find another job quite quickly. The good news was he would be working away from home a lot less. The bad news was that he would need to be based closer to his new employer, which meant them moving house and changing her daughter's school. And for Vicki, it would also mean leaving her job at Kismet. After much discussion, they decided they should go for it. And 5 Dillon Street marched on quietly in the background, with Vicki able to juggle her new day job, parenting, and occasionally travelling to the site to make sure she was on top of things. Luckily her professional team was proving to be worth their weight in gold. They'd made sure that the project was progressing, and she always looked forward to her weekly calls with her Project Manager.

One of her biggest revelations had been the unexpected friendship she'd struck up with Steve. He seemed genuinely excited about her project and would regularly call to learn how things were progressing. David told her it was because no one else had ever invited Steve and Natasha to dinner before, but she'd put it down to the near-magical powers of her mushroom linguine. And having spoken to Steve on numerous occasions, she'd found his guidance to be invaluable.

In the end, it took almost two years to the day, from her offer being accepted on Dillon Street to the sale proceeds arriving from her sixth and final flat. One of her favourite memories had been the day that she'd brought her husband and daughter to see the completed apartments for the first time. David was in total awe and couldn't believe she'd done it. He was so proud of her. And as she looked around at the beautiful new apartments, she wasn't quite sure she could believe it either.

Another very welcome arrival had been the £30k Development Management Fee that Vicki had been paid during the construction phase of the project. She was glad Steve had reminded her to check with her broker to make sure her lender offered this.

Three short months later, she received confirmation that the final sale proceeds were in her account. She'd managed to turn £10k into £240k in just two years. It had been frustrating and stressful and, at times, a bit scary. But it was easily the most fulfilling thing she'd ever done, and she couldn't wait to do it again. Yet a plan was beginning to formulate in her mind that she thought could dramatically change things for her and her family. She just needed to work out the numbers and think it all through.

Vicki's first development project: 5 Dillon Street

Purchase cost: £300k (of which £210k borrowed from commercial lender and £90k from private investors)

Purchase costs: £10k (funded by Vicki)

Development Costs: £350k (100% funded by the commercial lender)

GDV: £900k (what the flats were sold for)

Profit: £240k (including £30k Development Management Fee that Vicki was paid during the construction phase)

Timescale: 24 months

Tom had returned from the bar brandishing a second round of drinks and sat back down. Vicki's story had been amazing, and he was so happy that she'd managed to complete a development project successfully. But Dillon Street was, what, 17 years ago? What had she been up to since then?

Vicki explained that she'd gone on to do some more development projects. For a while, she'd considered stepping up in scale but then decided that it wasn't worth all the extra stress. There seemed to be a lot of scope to convert smaller commercial buildings and shops into flats, and at the small-scale end of the market, she wasn't competing with the larger developers. She'd also discovered that her second project had been a lot easier than her first. After all, she already had a great team, a proven track record with her private investors and commercial lenders, and good relationships with agents. Plus, she now had all that development experience under her belt that she had gained from her first project.

But that wasn't all. She had decided to adopt a second strategy in parallel with her property developing, one of which she was sure Tom would approve. She wanted to use the money she made from each project to build a buy-to-let portfolio.

Tom nodded his approval and couldn't resist asking Vicki how her portfolio was coming along. She explained that she'd bought three £200k rental properties with the profits from Dillon Street. This cost her £150k in deposits and £30k in fees, which left £70k to pay tax on her profits. She'd then gone on to do four other similar conversion projects over the next eight years. As soon as one development finished, she'd start on the next. These projects, on average, returned a £240k profit and took an average of two years to complete. This allowed her to buy three £200k rental units every 24 months using buy-to-let mortgages, with a 25% deposit on each, £10k in fees, and the remainder put aside for tax.

Vicki's Landlord Developer Strategy

Each Development Produced Profit of: £240k every 2 years, of which £150k was used as 25% deposits for 3 rental properties, with remainder used to pay taxes and acquisition costs

Total no. of developments completed:	5 in ten years
Total development profit:	£970k
Total rental properties bought:	15
Value of portfolio after 20 years:	£8.0m+
Less mortgages of:	£2.25m
Equity after 20 years:	£5.75m
Annual rental profit:	£100k+

Tom's head was swimming as he did the mental arithmetic. Did this mean that Vicki now had fifteen rental properties? Vicki nodded, smiling. She knew it sounded ridiculous. But doing those five small-scale developments had literally changed her life.

In fact, she'd decided to stop developing after the first ten years so she could spend more time with her family. Today, the portfolio was producing a healthy six-figure rental profit each year, plus her equity was growing by around £500,000 each year as well. If she sold the portfolio today, she'd realise nearly £5.8m in profit, which didn't seem like a bad return for converting a handful of small commercial buildings into flats over a decade ago.

Vicki saw Tom's stunned expression and couldn't resist another smile. She'd ended up copying Tom's own property strategy, yet because she'd taken on some developments as well, she'd managed to build a portfolio many times the size of his. And effectively retired after just ten years.

Tom shook his head in wonderment. He had to hand it to her; it was indeed an amazing story. He's right about that, Vicki thought to herself, then, checking her watch said she ought to be heading off home. They both donned their coats and headed out into cold, their breaths billowing in the cold, brightly lit street outside.

As they walked towards the building they'd met in earlier, Tom asked her how long she'd been working at the estate agents. Vicki laughed and shot him a puzzled look. What did he mean? She didn't work there. She'd only gone in there to sort out some paperwork with the branch manager. She explained she'd been asked to advise a friend of hers on a local development project they were looking at. The two of them had walked around the site first thing after lunch today and had then gone in to see the branch manager to finalise the deal. To be honest, she hadn't been at all sure about getting involved. But Steve was now a good friend, and he'd helped her out a lot in her early days. Plus, she quite liked the thought of giving him advice without having responsibility for putting it into effect. And, when she'd discovered it was the old Kismet building that Steve was going to convert, it seemed like, well...

As they reached Tom's car, he asked her if they could meet up again sometime. Maybe a family thing when it was warmer? Had he mentioned he was now something of a barbecue god and could do things with seasoned chicken that very few men were capable of?

Vicki laughed and rooted around in her bag for a business card, which she handed to him, suggesting he might want to avoid washing it this time, which prompted an embarrassed wince from Tom. She hugged him and told him not to leave it another twenty years before getting in touch. Then he watched as she climbed into her dark blue Range Rover and disappeared into the swirling snow of the late evening traffic.

5. A Reality Check

So, what did you make of our two protagonists? They both seemed to reach a happy ending through their property endeavours, but you have to hand it to Vicki. She completed just five small conversions and became a multi-millionaire, retiring after just ten years. And she started with an investment of just £10k, an amount that could well be within the reach of many.

Here are the final positions:

	Tom	Vicki
Equity after 20 years:	£1.3m	£5.75m
Annual rental profit:	£16k	£100k+

But how achievable is it in reality? Are you worried that we airbrushed the numbers and made the whole thing appear way too easy? Can you really turn £10k into £240k in two years? Or retire after only ten years having done just five small projects, with assets in the millions?

While the short answer is 'yes', before you say, 'where do I sign?', let's spend some time looking beneath the surface. The principles discussed in the story are entirely accurate; however, we need to explain some devils lurking in the detail. The purpose of this book is NOT to make you think property development is an absolute breeze. We happen to believe it's the easiest and quickest way of achieving financial freedom that there is, but that's NOT the same thing as saying that it's easy, far from it. But then you probably wouldn't expect something that can deliver that sort of financial result to be a complete walk in the park.

Property development involves getting educated, putting in some hard work, being tenacious, taking on a certain amount of risk, and being an entrepreneur. We've just given you a story that shows the sizzle on the sausage; what we now need to do is give you an understanding of what's involved in the journey, warts and all, so you can make up your own mind about whether you want to try and achieve it.

So, what did we miss out in our story about Tom and Vicki?

The first thing we skipped over in the story was the work the protagonists had to do to achieve their goals. While investing and developing can be done in your spare time, developing, in particular, involves a lot of effort, particularly at the start. By the end of this book, you'll have a good appreciation of the work involved, but we certainly didn't dwell on it in our story.

The second point is that not everyone who becomes a landlord or a developer is as successful as Tom and Vicki. Many variables can come into play, and those such as the economy and house price inflation are largely out of your control. The trick is to minimise as much of the risk as possible so that the chances of you not having a great outcome are minimised, something we'll talk about later.

Let's now look at some other factors that could have played a part in our story. We'll start with Tom.

The buy-to-let reality check

The first thing to mention is that we made some broad assumptions about fees in the quoted buy-to-let numbers. When you buy a property, there will be some fees to pay, including solicitor's fees and stamp duty, which will sit outside your mortgage. How much you pay can depend on several factors, including whether you purchase the property as an individual or through a company. This is important since it could be a significant number, perhaps as much as 10% of the cost of the property. In Tom and Vicki's case, we assumed that when buying each £200k buy-to-let, they paid £10k in fees; however, this figure could be higher or lower, depending on the circumstances.

We didn't factor in any refurbishment costs either. We suspect that many landlords will spend a small amount refreshing their new units before renting them out, but that isn't always the case. With Tom's first property, you'll recall he and Sandra redecorated it themselves. Not a huge expense, but we didn't include it.

We also applied a very broad brush to our inflationary assumptions. We had the value of Tom and Vicki's rental properties doubling every ten years and assumed that their rental profits increased by an underlying inflation rate of 2.5% per year. It's also worth mentioning that house prices aren't guaranteed to double every decade, but they have generally done so on average historically. There are certainly some reasons why they might not do so in the future, and we'll explore those later. Many variables can influence the value of a particular property, but we decided to go with the 'double every decade' as a general rule, plus it made the maths a lot easier ☺.

The keener-eyed reader may also have spotted that Tom bought his second property for the same price as his first (£200k), yet house prices had doubled in the ten-year intervening period. This must mean his second property was much smaller than his first or in a less valuable area (or both). Rental inflation rarely eclipses house price inflation. So, if you spend the same amount on a property purchase every ten years, you're likely to afford a smaller property each time you buy and will therefore receive lower rental profits in relative terms.

We took a reasonably broad-brush approach to taxation with our figures, as this could vary considerably. The £60k in rental profits that Tom earned during the first ten years would have been subject to tax, which would mean it would not then be wholly available to invest in his second property. But there is a range of scenarios here. What if the property was held in a company? What if Tom's wife, Sandra, had held the beneficial interest and the £4,800 annual profit was her only income and placed her in the 0% income tax band? What if Tom invested the profits and managed to offset some of the tax cost? In the final reckoning, we could always assume that Tom made up any shortfall through his savings or work salary. If he paid £10k in tax on the £60k rental profit he made, he would only need to find £1k per year to make up the shortfall by year ten. We're not sure that this would have affected his outcome too much.

Another somewhat variable omission would be any maintenance costs for the rental units. We'd allocated a small monthly reserve to pay for ongoing maintenance, but if there had been a significant outlay, it could have dented both Tom and Vicki's profits.

Finally, you'll have spotted that both used only their initial seed capital and their subsequent profits to build their portfolios. Tom (and Vicki) could have grown his portfolio more quickly had he invested cash from elsewhere (e.g. work savings or bonuses), but we wanted to demonstrate the comparison between a buy-to-let investor starting with £60k and a landlord developer starting with £10k, without any new money being invested.

So that was Tom's reality check. Now let's look at Vicki's.

The property development reality check

Some of Tom's reality check points apply equally to Vicki's own lettings portfolio so we won't repeat them here. But let's look at some of the issues that could have affected Vicki's development projects.

Perhaps one of the most significant question marks for anyone considering property development involves the amount of cash they're going to need. We're going to be doing a much deeper dive on that side of things later in the book, but let's first consider what happened to Vicki.

We've assumed that her Dillon Street project was similar to Steve's shop conversion in terms of the high-level numbers. To make the figures easier, we'd assumed that she needed a deposit of £90k in total but could borrow 100% of this from private investors. While some lenders are happy for the developer to borrow all of their deposits from private investors, others want the developer to invest some of their own money, so they have some skin in the game. If you're putting your own cash in, you'll have access to more lenders; however, it's certainly possible to find lenders who require no money in from the developer personally. Dillon Street cost £300k to purchase, with the commercial lender funding £210k and Vicki finding the remaining 30% (£90k) from private investors. Add in the £350k development finance, and it meant the entire project costs were £650k, of which Vicki contributed none of her own cash. In the end, she paid just £10k of her own money, which covered the stamp duty, survey, and solicitor's fees. If she'd not had £10k, she could have raised some additional private finance to pay for these costs.

This is one of the fundamental misconceptions about property development. Most people assume that you must need to stump up a lot of your own money to develop a project that produces a

£250k profit. What we've tried to demonstrate in our story is that Vicki had far less money than Tom and so couldn't afford to buy a buy-to-let property. But she could afford to become a property developer.

It's important to understand what other items you could be on the hook for, aside from your deposit. You generally have a lot more flexibility with private investors, with most being more concerned that you pay the money back with interest on the agreed date rather than the specifics of what you spend it on.

Here are a few examples of what you could be paying for that would sit outside the asset or development finance:

Stamp duty

This will be payable when you purchase the land or property you're going to develop. This could be a material amount; however, it could be included within the asset finance in certain cases. Where it isn't, you could fund it yourself or use private finance. We'd recommend discussing this with your commercial broker (we'll introduce the two of you later in the book ☺).

Professional fees

The development finance will pick up most fees associated with the project, so you won't have to pay for these yourself. But there could be instances where you need to get some plans drawn up in advance of the sale or have some due diligence work done by members of your professional team BEFORE you buy the property. This could include work done by your architect or your planning consultant. Many commercial lenders will allow you to claim back these fees from the first drawdown payment of the development finance, but you'll need to agree on this first, and of course, you'll need to pay the fees yourself before you get refunded in the first drawdown payment.

Conveyancing

Your solicitor will need paying, and their fee will sit outside the commercial finance.

Valuation fee

Your commercial lender will charge you a fee for having their surveyor value the land or property you're buying, and clearly, this will be payable before they lend you any money.

Branding

If you are new to development, you'll initially need to create a brand identity for yourself. This will enable you to create a significant amount of credibility from Day 1, and we'll be walking you through this later in the book. We're talking about creating a website, logo design, business cards, stationery, and the like. They won't cost a king's ransom but will likely run to a few hundred pounds.

Other due diligence costs

There are likely to be costs associated with finding a project initially and evaluating a project once you've found one. This could include optional software subscriptions that can help you evaluate sites more efficiently, paying a virtual assistant to help you do some of the grunt work, transport costs for traveling to potential sites to assess them, and setting up a limited company.

One of the most significant gaps in Vicki's budget related to training, and we didn't allocate any money to it in our story. You could argue that she had some support and advice from Steve that would have helped her, but for someone with zero property development experience, not getting any training is asking for trouble. Of course, it IS possible to develop property without getting trained, but as you can imagine, you'll likely fall down some holes and miss lots of opportunities since you won't know what you're doing. We'll talk about training in the last part of the book, but if you're serious about development, we'd recommend budgeting between £10k and £20k to get trained properly; it will pay for itself several times over.

If you're thinking that sounds like quite an investment, one way to rationalise the cost of training is to look at the profits that are being generated here. A £10k or £20k training cost is a fraction of the profit Vicki made from her first project, and when you look at her financial situation after twenty years, it's a drop in the ocean. Yet it can easily mean the difference between success and failure when you first start.

As with the rental profits, we were quite non-specific on the tax Vicki would pay on her development profits since it could vary significantly depending on how she set things up. We'll run through these options later in the book, but we did mention she had £70k set aside to pay the tax on the £240k profit she'd made from her first project. Is this realistic? Well, because her earnings would have been in a limited company, she'd have needed to pay corporation tax at 19%, which would be £45,600. This would leave her £24,400 left over to cover any other expenses, so we think setting aside £70k should be more than adequate. On her subsequent projects, she also averaged £240k profit which would give her the same £45,600 corporation tax bill, and we'd allowed £60k, so again, we think it sounds prudent.

It's worth noting that Vicki's commercial lender lent her 70% of the asset price and required her to contribute none of the deposit personally. While a 70% loan to value is commonplace, some lenders may offer a reduced loan to value or require a more significant developer contribution to the deposit. We'll be discussing this in more detail later, but you should note that it's not cast in stone.

A further thought on Vicki's situation is that she could have chosen to take on a smaller project and still made a healthy six-figure profit. If she'd targeted a £100k profit from each deal, this would have required a GDV of around £500k and a likely asset purchase price (the price paid for the building to be converted) of approximately £200k. Assuming a 70% loan to value, Vicki's total deposit would have been £60k, and her cash contribution would have been less than £10k. These are ball-park numbers, but they demonstrate the low cost of entry compared with purchasing a buy-to-let property, where a 25% deposit is typically required, which will usually be your own cash.

Finally, Vicki could have decided to up her workload, and work on two projects simultaneously, each starting 12 months apart i.e., staggered. Since the work involved by the developer typically reduces when a project starts on site, Vicki could have used this time to find and start another project. Had she done this, she would have had a new two-year project starting every 12 months rather than every 24 months, which would have added another 80% or so to her final equity and rental profit position after 20 years.

Hopefully, Tom and Vicki's story has given you an insight and maybe even a little inspiration. Now, we promised earlier that we'd take a closer look at the pros and cons of a development strategy versus going down the rental route, so let's do that now.

Ian Child & Ritchie Clapson

6. Landlord or Developer?

The traditional landlord's route

In our Tom and Vicki story, we highlighted the impact that development can have on a property investor's fortunes, but in this chapter, it's worth circling back to make sure we've nailed the detail. You could become a landlord, a developer, neither, or both, and it's essential to understand the pros and cons of each route, which is the primary purpose of this chapter.

The landlord's lot used to be a happy one. The story would typically unfold like this; you would buy a house or flat, usually using a buy-to-let mortgage. You'd put down a deposit of, say, 25%, and the bank would lend you the rest. Then, you'd find a tenant or two who would pay you rent, and because the rental income is greater than your mortgage repayments, you'd make a rental profit. And in the background, the value of your house or flat would slowly grow in value over time, as house prices generally do.

This equity growth may be slow, but it's quite sexy for two reasons. Firstly, house price increases have been relatively dependable. Yes, property values can go down as well as up, but over the long-term, they've proved to be reliable. As we mentioned, historically, you could hang your hat on the fact that property values in the UK will double roughly every ten years or so on average, and you don't have to do anything other than wait; it will happen automatically without you having to lift a finger (we'll refer to this doubling every ten years as the "Doubling Effect")

That said, there is currently some speculation that the Doubling Effect might be a thing of the past. Between 2011 and 2021, house prices in the UK increased on average by just 53%. This in itself isn't a problem since we know that the Doubling Effect is an average over many decades, not a guaranteed result for the current decade. Yet many believe that house price inflation of this magnitude may not be sustainable over the next few decades due to economic factors and possible government intervention. The government has a conundrum to deal with. Robust house price inflation is the sign of a strong economy, yet where these increases are greater than people's earnings, it makes it increasingly difficult for them to get on the housing ladder. Between 2011 and 2021, earnings rose less than 30% compared to house prices which, as you now know, rose 53%. At some point, this gap could increase to such an extent that most people will have to abandon any hope of ever owning their own home. Understandably this is something that politicians are keen to avoid. There's every prospect that the government could suppress house price inflation to well below the 100% per decade needed to sustain the Doubling Effect. For buy-to-let landlords, it means that their long-term portfolio equity growth could be substantially less than they'd planned or hoped for.

The power of financial leverage as a landlord

As we've already mentioned, one of the sexier parts of the buy-to-let model is the financial leverage you get from the bank's money (the buy-to-let mortgage). It's the point that Tom's wife Sandra made when they were buying property number two. You may have only contributed 25% of the acquisition cost of your rental property (the deposit), but you'll receive 100% of any uplift in its value. The poor old bank doesn't get to share in any of this equity growth –

you get it all (this is the only time we'll refer to banks as being poor, we promise ☺).

Let's remind ourselves of Tom's example to demonstrate the point. He bought a house for £200k using a buy-to-let mortgage. He put down a deposit of 25%, which is £50k, and the bank lent him the remaining £150k as a buy-to-let mortgage (we'll ignore things like fees, interest, and stamp duty, for now, to keep things simple). Then, without him having to do a great deal, the property slowly but surely increased in value to the extent that, after ten years (or so), it had doubled in value and was now worth £400k. If he'd decided to sell the property at this point, he'd have received £400k, but he would still owe the bank £150k, which means his initial investment of £50k has turned into a cool £250k. The house has doubled in value, but his equity has increased five-fold. He's simply used the bank's share of the property as leverage to get more profit for himself.

This is why buy-to-let mortgages, even though they involve borrowing money, are a 'good' debt to have because they allow you to leverage the bank's capital to create greater wealth for yourself. If Tom had used his £50k to buy a (very cheap!) property for £50k with no mortgage, then the property would still have doubled in value, but Tom's equity would only have increased to £100k, instead of £250k.

The power of financial leverage as a developer

As a property developer, financial leverage is still taking place but in a slightly different way and on a much larger scale.

Using Vicki as an example, she was able to generate £240k profit for herself in two years by investing just £10k. Yes, she did more work than Tom, but Tom took ten years to reach £250k from a £60k investment, whereas she got to the same £250k position with a sixth of the initial investment and in a fifth of the time. It's quite literally in a different league, and we don't know of another property investment strategy that comes anywhere close to being able to produce this scale of return so quickly.

The leverage in development comes from both the commercial lending that finances 70% of the asset cost and 100% of the development cost and the private investment that makes up some or all of the deposit. The key difference between the two models is that Tom's equity growth relies on house prices increasing over the long term, whereas Vicki's equity growth comes from using development to force value into a property or piece of land in the short term.

The additional magic in Vicki's model occurs because, despite this improved leverage, there are no losers. The private investors and commercial lenders who lend the money get a great return, and the professionals who build the projects get a healthy fee for their troubles. And, of course, the developer gets the biggest profit of all. The people who buy the property always pay the market rate, so they're not losing out. And the person who sold the property to the developer wouldn't have been able to develop it (else they would have done so), so they sold it at a fair price. A virtuous circle that only comes to pass because the developer decides to develop.

Maximising rental income

Ok, so that's equity growth taken care of, but what about the other side of the landlord's business model, which is rental income? Again, there's no rocket science involved here. Both Tom and Vicki found tenants to live in their properties, and they paid them rent. Again, let's remind ourselves of the numbers.

Tom was getting £1,000 per month in rent but then had to make a buy-to-let mortgage payment of £400. Then he must pay fees to a letting agent, buy some insurance and set aside some funds for running repairs and maintenance. There will be an annual gas safety inspection and some PAT testing on any electrical appliances. We assumed these overheads cost him £200 per month, which left Tom with a profit of £400.

It's worth noting that had Tom not needed a mortgage and bought the property with his own cash, he would still have the £200 monthly overhead costs, but he'd have no mortgage payments to make. As a result, he'd be making £800 profit per month instead of £400. On the flip side, he would have had to invest another £150k of his own money to do it, plus his equity would only double every ten years rather than increasing five-fold. Personally, we prefer the more leveraged approach.

But both Tom and Vicki arguably missed a trick when it came to maximising the profits from their rental units. There's a more lucrative way of configuring buy-to-let properties so that they generate more income than a single let. If Tom had converted his first 3-bedroomed house into a house of multiple occupation (HMO), he could have created a property with four separate bedrooms that share a bathroom, kitchen, and lounge. He could then rent each room out to four separate tenants, for example, some young professionals. So instead of having one single family paying rent of £1,000 per month, he'd have four tenants each paying £400, a total of £1,600 per month. Depending on the configuration of the property, he may even have managed to create a five or six-bedroomed HMO.

On the flip side, he'd probably have to pay more on the upkeep of each property, as four separate young people are likely to wear things out more quickly than a family would. Plus, he'll pay more in letting fees. And, of course, he'd have had to spend money upfront to convert the properties he bought into HMOs.

Ultimately, HMOs are a great way of increasing your profits from a rental property, albeit they are more likely to have voids, although not for the entire property. They will also take more effort and expense to set up and maintain. But we felt it was important to mention them because they certainly should be considered by anyone looking at a buy-to-let investment model. In fact, there's a multitude of different rental-related strategies that can generate significantly better returns than a straightforward buy-to-let, and it's worth getting yourself educated about them if that's a path you're considering.

The landlord's old challenges

But, as we mentioned in the opening chapter, being a buy-to-let landlord isn't all a bed of roses for several reasons. The first is that you'll need to find tenants to live in your property. Without these, you'll have no rental income from which to pay your mortgages. And once you've found your tenants, you'll need to look after them. Yes, you can pay for a lettings agency to find you tenants, collect rent, and manage your property; however, you won't be able to divest yourself of being ultimately responsible for your portfolio. You have both a legal and moral responsibility to be a decent landlord, and this means staying on top of the ever-increasing amount of legislation that protects tenants.

You'll also need to maintain a slush fund for unexpected expenses since these can often come out of the blue and will need sorting immediately. Broken boilers are rarely cheap to repair, and your tenants won't be able to wait for you to save up your pennies until you're flush enough to afford it.

And being a hands-off landlord comes at quite a premium. You can end up giving away a fair slice of your profits paying for letting agencies to find and vet tenants, manage your properties, attend to (some of) your legal responsibilities, and undertake any maintenance or repair jobs.

The landlord's new challenges

So, you have ongoing responsibilities and operational costs as a landlord, but this won't come as a major shock. Perhaps more surprising, as we alluded to earlier, are some of the government's changes in recent years that have significantly dented the appeal of becoming a landlord in the first place and, in many cases, forced some landlords to sell their portfolios and quit the business altogether.

The first recent change came in 2016, when the then Chancellor of the Exchequer, George Osbourne, announced that there was to be an additional 3% stamp duty to be paid on any residential property purchase that was not your main residence. This additional burden was on top of the standard stamp duty that would otherwise apply, and clearly, second homeowners and landlords were the primary victims. Assuming the average property cost £200,000, landlords would suddenly be faced with an additional £6,000 upfront cost when starting their portfolio or adding to it.

In the same year, Osbourne announced a further change that would profoundly affect many existing landlords, namely a change in the tax law that affects the amount of tax relief that landlords receive. A new Section 24 of the Finance Act 2015 was phased in gradually and came into full effect in April 2020. Prior to Section 24, landlords could deduct mortgage interest from their income tax bill, plus they could deduct other related costs such as mortgage admin fees. However, Section 24 means they now need to pay tax on ALL the rental income they receive. They would be able to claim this back, but only up to the basic rate of income tax. Not only does this mean that landlords now pay more tax upfront when they buy a property, those that are higher-rate taxpayers will pay more tax on their rental income too.

As an example, Nicholas is a basic-rate taxpayer whose annual rental income is £15,000 with his mortgage interest being £5,000. Kathy is a higher-rate tax payer and has identical rental income and mortgage interest to Nicholas. Both will pay tax on the full rental income, which means Nicholas's tax bill will be £3,000 (20%) and Kathy's will be £6,000 (40%). Similarly, both can claim back 20% of their interest payments which is £1,000 (20% of £5,000). This means that Nicholas's net tax cost is £2,000 and Kathy's is £5,000. Prior to Section 24, Nicholas's tax cost would have been £2,000 and Kathy's would have been £4,000. The impact of Section 24 is therefore minimal for basic rate tax payers but potentially significant for those paying higher-rate tax, and it understandably became a significant challenge for landlords with larger portfolios.

At this point, it's worth noting that Section 24 only applies to personal income tax. Buy-to-let properties owned by limited companies are not affected, however they ARE subject to Capital Gains Tax and Corporation Tax (so make sure to get advice from a good property accountant if you intend to start a rental portfolio). Today many new buy-to-let purchases are made by landlords buying through a company rather than as individuals.

Problem solved for everyone, then? Not quite. You see, for those landlords that already owned rental properties, while they had the option to transfer their portfolio into a new limited company to avoid Section 24, this transfer would crystallise a capital gain. Since they and their limited company are separate legal entities, the transfer is effectively a sale of the property from entity A (themselves) to entity B (their new company). As a result, entity A would get taxed on any capital gain since it acquired the property. For landlords who had bought their properties many years ago, this equity gain was significant and meant that transferring to a company-owned portfolio model would create a huge tax bill.

Has the government now finished targeting landlords with regulation changes or tax hikes? We think we can safely predict that the answer to that question is 'no'. The problem that landlords have is that they are a relatively wealthy yet small subset of the population, plus they don't tend to garner much public sympathy (despite the critical role they play in ensuring people have homes to live in, but don't get us started...). As a result, most landlords can afford to pay more tax without falling into poverty, and there won't be a public outcry if the government targets them.* Nor will many votes be lost because there are only 2.65m landlords in the UK, which is only 5% or so of the voting population (plus they tend not to switch their political allegiance just because the government taxes them harder).

Whatever your political views, it would be naïve to think that landlords won't be targeted again at some point, whichever party is in power.

Interestingly, the Private Landlords Survey published by the Ministry of Housing, Communities and Local Government in 2019 showed that 94% of landlords in England operate as private individuals rather than as companies. They earn on average £15,000 before tax and other deductions, with rents making up 42% of their gross income. 59% of landlords were over 55, and a third were retired. Many of these landlords hold equity in their rental properties; however, it gives an interesting perspective on how wealthy the average landlord might be. Of course, there are some super-wealthy landlords, but this government survey would suggest that the majority are not.

The path not taken

We've looked at the role of a traditional buy-to-let landlord, and for most people, this is the only route into property that they ever consider. So, why don't they look at property development as an alternative?

The main challenge of property development is that it looks risky and complicated. Buying a house and renting it out is something that most people can get their heads around, and after all, how difficult can it be? It all sounds relatively hands-off, and aside from the odd tenant issue and maintenance bill, it must surely be a breeze in comparison to building a property from scratch? Plus, of course, property tends to appreciate over time, so the chances of your investment going down as a landlord must be relatively small compared to being a developer. Also, many new landlords know people who are existing landlords, so it feels like a much more comfortable step to take.

The other perception is that being a landlord is effectively an investment strategy, whereas being a property developer sounds more like a job or career. And if you've already got a job (or are not looking for another one), then surely you won't want to become a developer.

So, several very plausible reasons why people choose the landlord route over the development one, and in many respects, they're not wrong. However, there's a little more to it than a first glance would suggest, and as a result, there's more opportunity. After all, pursuing a strategy that other investors aren't looking at often provides the best results – just ask Warren Buffet. Let's then look at what's involved in being a small-scale developer.

Introducing small-scale property development

When many people think of property development, they imagine new housing estates or shopping centres, with lots of tall cranes and hundreds of people milling about in hard hats and hi-vis jackets. While this is still property development, it's on a much larger scale than we'll be talking about in this book. While a developer can start small and then build up to these larger-scale projects, it's by no means essential to do so, and in fact, there's a powerful argument to suggest that going large in development terms is a bad idea due to the 'expansion syndrome' we talked about earlier.

So, what do we mean when we say 'small-scale'?

Let's start by giving you a different perspective on the term 'property development'. At a fundamental level, it simply means adding value to a building or piece of land. So, if you buy a 'doer-upper', give it a lick of paint, put in a new kitchen and bathroom, and then flip it on a few months later for a cool £40k profit, then this is property development. Similarly, if you're a landlord who buys a tired three-bed semi and converts it into a five-bed HMO, then this too constitutes developing property, even if you don't sell it and just keep it to rent out. If you self-build, then you're a developer. You could even argue that improving your own home constitutes property development; you may not get the financial return immediately, but the value of your property has gone up because of the work you've undertaken.

If this sounds like something you've done before, then congratulations on being a property developer already! Ok, it's not quite the type of development we're going to be covering in this book, but hopefully, it makes the point that property development sits on a scale with building housing estates at one end and sprucing up a tired flat at the other. The small-scale projects we'll be talking about sit much closer to a small 'flip' end of the scale; they're effectively the next step up. If you were previously thinking you couldn't become a property developer because you could never envisage yourself building a housing estate, then instead, we want you to think, 'I could easily become a small-scale developer because it's only one step up from renovating a flat or house.'

That leverage principle (again)

But hold on a moment, we hear you say. If a small flip would net me, say, £40k profit, it sounds like quite a big jump up to a range of between £100k and £500k. Are you sure that small-scale development really is the next step up?

It's a fair question, so let us explain. First, let's look at what a medium-scale development would produce, profit-wise. Assuming an average house value of £200k and a margin of 20%, building 30 houses would equate to a £6m GDV and a profit of £1.2m. While this may sound like a significant development from your perspective, it's relatively small in development terms, yet the profit is still several times greater than we'd expect from a small-scale project. So, our £100k minimum doesn't look unreasonable when we look at it in the context of other sizes of project.

However, the biggest factor in extending the scope of your profits from £40k to £100k+ is our good friend leverage again. This time though, it's not financial leverage but the leverage of resources. This benefit occurs because of the difference in scale between a simple flip and a small-scale development project.

When people flip property, create an HMO, or spruce up a rental, they're typically going to have a relatively small budget. It will vary quite a bit, but let's say the budget was £30k. The other thing that happens with this type of project is that you typically oversee the work yourself. That's not to say you'd be on-site 24/7, but you're likely to be popping round reasonably frequently to make sure that work was progressing on a timely basis, that the quality was up to scratch and that things were generally going according to plan. You're also likely to have appointed a builder to do the work and maybe some other tradespeople as well, and if you were a dab hand at the old DIY, then, who knows, you may also be getting your hands dirty yourself. After all, your time effectively comes for free, which means more profit at the end of the day.

Now let's look at a small-scale development by way of contrast. We'll assume the project sits at the smaller end of the scale at £600k GDV, with a target profit of £120k. The first thing to notice is that the construction cost will be way bigger than with the flip. We would typically expect construction costs (materials and labour) to account for between 33% and 40% of the GDV, and so if we assume the lower end of the scale, this will give us a construction budget of £200k. This compares to a budget of just £30k for the flip and places us in a different league.

There are two key reasons why this is important. The first is that we can afford to engage the service of a main contractor. A main contractor will be a much larger enterprise than a jobbing builder, and critically for you, they have responsibility for delivering every aspect of the construction. On a flip, you can't afford a main contractor, and you might bring in several other subcontractors yourself to pick up specific tasks, in addition to the role of your builder. There's also an argument that a main contractor has more resources available and can deliver a better overall quality.

The second significant benefit of this step-up in budget is that you can afford to hire a Project Manager. This is a game-changer, so let's explain exactly why.

The role of the Project Manager

The role of the Project Manager or PM is to oversee the construction phase of a development project. On your flip project, YOU would be the person going to the site, checking on progress, chivvying up your builder, and discussing design challenges with your architect. On small-scale development, that role would be performed by a Project Manager. They will act as your eyes and ears on the ground and will have a great deal of experience in making sure that things go to plan and that the other team members deliver precisely what's required.

Another massive advantage of a PM is that they have a great deal more experience managing construction projects (and contractors) than you do, and as a result, they're much better at it. Unsurprisingly, most new developers feel somewhat daunted by the prospect of running a project on-site. After all, they're surrounded by people who have more experience than they do and who could easily pull the wool over their eyes. This ceases to be a problem with a PM since they have the expertise that you lack. They'll go to the site regularly to check on progress, issue instructions to the team, and report back to you. Plus, they're going to be wise to most of the tricks of the trade so that they can protect your bottom line. They'll refer any decision-making to you as necessary and will often make recommendations. You don't even need to visit the site yourself (although we would strongly recommend that you show your face occasionally).

In short, PMs are one of the main reasons that you can run your development as a hands-off CEO, and they will be critical to your success as a developer.

A magical combination

The final concept we want to cover in this chapter is one we've already introduced through Vicki's story, namely the idea that you can be both a property developer AND a buy-to-let investor at the same time. In fact, this is such a great idea, we're amazed they don't teach it in schools. Why is it such a good strategy? Well, as you saw, it allows you to supercharge your portfolio growth and your profits in relatively short timescales.

Clearly, property developers have no absolute requirement to invest their profits in buy-to-let property. They could invest in the stock market, put it into a pension, or use it to finance future projects. Or they could simply spend it on nice cars and fancy holidays; the choice is entirely up to them. But remember the worry that Vicki had about her family's financial future; working in a supermarket in your dotage seems like a far cry from where you are today, but the money-go-round stops when you stop working. You then need to rely on passive income to maintain the lifestyle you want and, of course, to be able to afford some of life's more depressingly predictable things, such as deteriorating health and a need for end-of-life care for you and your partner. For many, there is also the consideration of leaving a financial legacy to children and grandchildren. And, of course, you can't decide to think about creating a pension or passive income when you retire; you have to do it while you're still working.

The other important consideration here is for those who are already landlords. We've already speculated that future equity growth may not revert to the Doubling Effect, at least for the next few decades. For those who look to remortgage their properties to fund new deposits, this could result in a significant delay in their portfolio growth. One of the key challenges that Tom experienced was that his portfolio grew at a snail's pace compared to Vicki's, and that was <u>with</u> property prices doubling every decade. It took him ten years to buy his second property, whereas Vicki had acquired fifteen properties in the same time frame (<u>and</u> she started investing two years <u>after</u> he did). After 20 years, Tom was only getting £16k in rental profits each year, which isn't particularly life-changing. Vicki, on the other hand, was making rental profits of over £100k.

One of the key advantages of building your portfolio earlier is that you benefit from supercharged equity growth. After twenty years, Vicki's equity was growing at over £500k per annum, and this was because she'd managed to build an extensive portfolio during the first ten of those years. Tom was entering his third decade with just three properties, albeit he was about to buy three more. Not only did he have far fewer properties, but his portfolio was also less mature, and so his equity had less time to grow.

Another key thought for existing landlords is this; many of you will have already updated and improved properties in your portfolio. Whether putting in new kitchens and bathrooms or converting a residential house into an HMO, you have effectively developed property. Commercial lenders see this as a big plus point because it means you already have experience in overseeing a development project. You've done the numbers, acquired the property, sorted the finance, overseen the changes, and then let it out, having increased its value in the process. Guess what? That's no different from the process you'd adopt with a small-scale development. So, if you're thinking you've done a refurb or an HMO conversion but aren't sure whether you're up to tackling a small-scale development, you might want to think again. Commercial lenders seem to think you can, and trust us; they're not in the business of taking any risk if they can help it.

In summary

In Part 1, we've looked to explain WHY small-scale property development might be a highly attractive option for you. Hopefully, we've given you a fresh perspective on development, particularly now that there is not only more opportunity than ever before but also that it represents a compelling alternative to other forms of wealth creation. The scenarios where development could be particularly appealing are:

- If you don't have enough cash to put down a deposit on a buy-to-let, you could do a development which would give you several deposits over say a 24-month period
- If you're a landlord who wants to grow your portfolio, development can help you achieve this much more quickly
- If you combine both a rental and development strategy, you can take your results into the stratosphere
- If you simply want to get involved in property investment and are looking for a rising market

Now, before we look at the mechanics of developing property, it's worth understanding the opportunities that currently exist for new developers operating at the small-scale end of the market. We mentioned earlier that several converging factors had created a surge in interest in property development recently, but there has also been a significant increase in the scope of development opportunities available generally. This has been brought about by a series of events that have been entirely unprecedented, a 'perfect storm' that has created the ideal opportunity for new developers to enter the market. So that's where we'll be heading in Part 2.

Part 2

What Should I Build?

Ian Child & Ritchie Clapson

7. The Perfect Storm

A wide range of factors influence the demand for property. Recently, we have seen a coming together of several elements that, when combined, have had a significant impact on the opportunities presented to property developers, particularly those looking to do smaller projects. In fact, we'd describe it as something of a 'perfect storm'.

Let's go through each of them individually so that we can see the state of the market and where the biggest opportunities are, starting with the current national housing stock.

The national housing shortage

Ever since most people can remember, there has been a housing shortage in the UK, and in recent years the government has reiterated that we need to be building over 300,000 new homes every year to try and catch up with demand. Compare this to the 170,000 or so homes built in 2019 in what was considered a bumper year (there were far fewer built in 2020 due to the coronavirus pandemic), you can see that a step change is needed. While even the most ambitious small-scale developer isn't going to make much of a dent in this number, it's worth understanding the impact that this underlying demand has on small-scale development from a business case perspective.

The primary question for any new business is a simple one; is there a demand for its products? Many businesses struggle with this issue, and quite often, what sounds like a great idea in principle can end up being a total flop when it's unleashed on the world at large. As a property developer, one gets to dodge this bullet simply because the underlying demand for housing is undeniable. That's not to say you can build anything anywhere and always guarantee a healthy profit. But with an intelligent approach and some sound local knowledge, you can be reasonably assured that someone will want to buy what you're selling. This may seem obvious, but it's not a luxury that every business has by a long chalk.

The old adage, of course, holds true; they're not making any more land. But we're still creating more people, and they all need somewhere to live. If you're in the business of building homes, then whatever level you're at, you're serving a very needy market.

The government's agenda

For some years now, the national housing shortage has been the subject of much consternation and gnashing of teeth in Whitehall's corridors of power. The underlying lack of what, after all, is one of society's fundamental requirements is not exactly a vote-winner, and not surprisingly, politicians are keen to find a solution.

Equally unsurprisingly, it turns out there's not a simple answer to the problem. Knocking up 300,000 new homes by creating a handful of new towns somewhere dotted around the country sounds easy when you say it quickly. But to put it into context, that's more than the number of houses that exist in the whole of Leicestershire or Oxfordshire. So, not only do we need to have a county's worth of new homes built every year, but we also need them to be built where the demand is, and not in inconvenient, out-of-the-way locations.

The other harsh reality is that most voters want these new homes to be built, providing they're not built anywhere near where they live. And if anyone suggests that our precious green belt should be built on, politicians can almost see the votes evaporating away. So, the answer, whatever it is, must be found in a more subtle way.

Permitted Development Rights (PDRs)

The government's housing dilemma leads us neatly on to the rise and rise of Permitted Development Rights (PDRs). We'll cover PDRs in more detail later, but for now, let's give you an overview. PDRs can trace their roots back to the 1940s, but in 2015, they had something of a renaissance.

The default position for changing the use of a building or erecting an extension or new build structure is that full planning permission (FPP) is required. Planning applications are made to and assessed by local planning authorities (LPAs), i.e., the local council's planning team. However, obtaining FPP is a complex, often time-consuming (and sometimes wholly nightmarish) process. The government acknowledges that there are situations where FPP would be overkill, for example, building a small extension on your home. As a result, they have given us PDRs that allow us to extend our homes within specific parameters without notifying anyone or asking for permission – we can just go ahead and do it.

There are also scenarios where the government wants to encourage buildings to be repurposed, for example, converting a disused or unwanted commercial building into much-needed residential units. All buildings have an allocated use class, and typically FPP would be required to change a use class from, say, retail to residential. However, the government has introduced PDRs that allow this change of use without the need to apply for FPP. This makes converting properties to residential using PDRs simpler, less risky, and much quicker. In short, then, PDRs are a blessing for developers.

However, unlike home extensions, the government acknowledges that these change of use PDRs may require a handful of checks and balances to be in place to prevent anything unsuitable from being built. After all, there may be some fundamental concerns, such as a lack of natural light or proximity to noisy factories that could make a conversion undesirable. As a result, for most change of use PDRs, developers will need to apply for what's known as Prior Approval to the council. This is not as comprehensive as FPP, but it still allows the council to reject an application if there are some fundamental concerns. Luckily, under the Prior Approval process, the list of areas on which the LPA can object are relatively small in number. This means you will usually know whether you meet those criteria BEFORE you commit to buy the property, rather than leaving it in the lap of the gods.

This PDR process is a gift for small-scale developers looking to convert existing buildings. The government has dramatically ramped up the use of PDRs over the last couple of years to try and encourage small developers to convert unwanted brownfield sites into residential and help plug the housing gap. Arguably the most draconian of all PDRs (called class MA) only came into effect in August 2021, causing an unprecedented volume of commercial properties to suddenly become convertible without FPP.

We'll be talking about this in more detail very soon, but for now, just note that these PDRs are fantastic news for small-scale, first-time developers, as they make developments quicker and less risky.

The impact of Covid-19

The world became a different place when Covid arrived, and we suspect things will not go completely back to 'normal' for some time, if ever. So how did the pandemic affect property development, and what will be its legacy?

Two factors have made a big difference. The first was the arrival of homeworking as a default arrangement. Entire workforces suddenly found themselves working from home, and employers were forced to accept homeworking as standard practice. This caused two things to happen. Firstly, having invested in a homeworking infrastructure, many employers saw the attraction of downsizing their expensive city centre offices and asking staff to come into work only one or two days a week. This, in turn, leads to a demand for smaller offices and a significant amount of the existing commercial property space becoming surplus to requirements. Given that much of this stock has PDRs, there is an opportunity to convert a lot of it to residential.

But this move to flexible working (part home/part office) had another significant impact. Some employees now needed to work from home for one or more days; however, for many, this was far from ideal, logistically. In theory, you were in a good place if you had a home office, but what if you worked off the kitchen table? Or what if you had a young family at home all day giving you zero privacy and refusing to make you cups of tea?

Then there was the issue of work separation. People like having a separate place of work because it allows them to separate their work and home lives. If you work at home all the time, you never really get a sense of switching off from work – you feel like you're in your place of work all day.

As a result, employees demanded local office space, flexible office spaces, and office 'pods' that they could commute to locally on their work-from-home days. This space could be rented using an allowance from their employer, or it could be bought outright. It was the ideal solution; only a short commute from home, yet it meant that home ceased to be a work environment.

Intriguingly, employers also saw the benefit of these local office 'hubs'. Instead of having everyone commute to the city every day, they could buy or rent regional hubs in different areas. This gave their workforce the ability to have a local commute on some days and a longer commute to a downsized central head office.

Homeworking also meant that employees were less tied to urban areas. If you're commuting into town every day, then you'll want to live nearby to reduce your commuting time. But if you're only going in once or twice a week, then why not live a bit further out where property is cheaper, and you get more for your money? Sure, you'll need to put up with a longer commute, but it's now only a couple of times a week.

This led to yet another impact of the pandemic; people decided that they wanted more space and, if possible, a garden. Spending lockdown in a flat wasn't much fun, and it emphasised the importance of having an outside space to swing cats and generally maintain one's sanity. At the same time, home office space became highly desirable, as did having super-fast wi-fi.

So, on the one hand, we have more buildings becoming available for conversion. On the other, we have a new demand for a different type of office building in local communities, all of which creates opportunities for developers.

The commercial real estate market

Small-scale development using PDRs requires a stock of convertible buildings, and these buildings tend to be owned or tenanted by SMEs (Small or Medium-sized Enterprises, a.k.a. small businesses). When we encounter challenges in the broader economy as we have done in the recent past, we inevitably see an increase in the failure of these businesses and, therefore, an increase in the number of properties becoming available. It may be that an owner-occupier is shutting up shop or downsizing or that a landlord is losing a tenant. Either outcome can lead to a potential opportunity for the building to become available for sale.

Not only has the most recent period been turbulent from an economic perspective, but we've also seen the pandemic create enormous challenges for SMEs. Bounce-back loans and a furlough scheme went a long way to protecting many businesses temporarily from having to face the harsh realities of survival. But when furloughing stopped and the loans started to become repayable, the tide went out, and we got to see which businesses were still viable. Many more will likely fail as the realities of a post-pandemic economy start to bite, which again will lead to more conversion opportunities becoming available, often from highly motivated sellers.

The opportunity for smaller developers

At face value, you'd have thought that the long-term national housing shortage would be a boon for the large and mid-size housebuilders, and of course, in many respects, it is. However, most brownfield sites (sites that have previously been developed) aren't attractive propositions for the big boys, who need to leverage their economies of scale. They don't usually get out of bed for anything less than a seven or eight-figure profit, and so the prospect of converting a shop or small office building is not appealing in the slightest – it simply won't make them enough money.

Large-scale homebuilders like to use a cookie-cutter model. Visit any large development site, and you'll often see the same house designs being built in each one. There's the 4-bed 'Grantham', the 3-bed 'Oxford', the 2-bed 'Churchill' and so on. This makes perfect sense; recycling good designs and using them all over the country is highly cost-effective. And, of course, you have a workforce who is familiar with building a standard product. Converting existing properties is very different because the developer is forced to create a new, unique solution for the building in question. This doesn't suit larger housebuilders, nor is it their core skillset. But it's perfect for small-scale developers whose business model is based on creating individual solutions rather than a more generic approach. Some brownfield sites will appeal to larger developers, but these tend to be larger sites where it's cost-effective to demolish what's there and then build their standard designs.

As a small-scale developer, knowing how to sweat the asset is important. If you can see how to create greater value from a conversion opportunity than the other people looking at it, you'll have a better chance of winning it. This is where having a good property education comes in. With a bit of knowledge and the benefit of someone else's experience, it's relatively easy to learn the tips and tricks that allow you to unlock the hidden value in properties that other people may have overlooked.

The new-look High Street

The country's High Streets have changed out of all recognition from their heyday, and many are now at a low point. Our shopping habits have primarily driven the change. First, the out-of-town supermarkets came along and put many local retailers out of business. The butcher, the baker, and the greengrocer all went from being stalwarts of the local retail community to counters in Tesco (the candlestick maker threw in the towel even earlier ☺). Convenience, choice, and value, plus free parking, made it impossible for most of them to compete.

Then the internet came along and pretty much finished the job. There's almost nothing that can't be bought from online retailers, and it's far more convenient than scouring the local town centre looking for what you want. Plus, you can get next-day delivery on most items. As a result, most town centres are a shadow of their former selves, often just a mix of coffee bars, vape stores, and charity shops. Perfect if you fancy a quiet puff over a cappuccino while wearing someone else's trousers, but otherwise, there aren't too many reasons to venture in.

However, change is on the horizon. The government is adamant that town centres will be rejuvenated, and it's trying to make it as easy as possible for this to happen. The key lies in increasing the number of people who physically live near the centre. This can be done by converting some of the redundant commercial and retail buildings into residential using PDRs. Once people start living in good quality houses and apartments in and around High Streets, this automatically creates a demand for other products and services in the town. Convenience stores, cafes, bars, restaurants, entertainment venues, and gyms will follow. This then attracts the boutiques; unique artisan stores selling various products such as clothing, jewellery, homeware, and furniture. Suddenly the town centre has ceased to be a coffee franchise and charity shop ghetto and has instead become a shopping and entertainment destination, a place people WANT to travel to, to spend time eating, browsing, and being entertained.

Spearheading this transition are the PDRs that allow us to convert shops and other commercial buildings in our town centres into residential homes. So, the high street now represents one of the biggest areas of opportunity for development.

Co-retail

Picture an old Debenhams department store languishing unwanted and unloved on one of the UK's many high streets. A relic of a bygone retail era, it's no longer suited to today's retail environment, as we explained in the previous section. But as a building, it still has the potential to serve the high street of the future.

One of the more recent phenomena on the 'new' high street has been the resurgence of what we've termed 'co-retail'. This is where various retailers rent or buy space in a single building. It harks back to the concept of bazaars and indoor markets. With an influx of cafés and boutiques, it makes perfect sense for smaller businesses to house themselves in a larger building surrounded by similar retailers. They create a collective draw that's greater than the sum of their parts, plus the overheads will be cheaper than operating a standalone store.

You can see how that old Debenham's department store would be ripe for conversion to co-retail. It's slap-bang in the middle of town and already has much of the infrastructure in place, such as escalators, stairwells, fire escapes, and toilets. There could also be scope to pop some flats or even hotel rooms on the upper floors to create a mixed-use development.

Not surprisingly, many such ideas are being discussed for these larger buildings all over the country; however, the same concept can apply to much smaller buildings. Yes, they require a minimum amount of floor space to house multiple retailers, but for the more speculative developer, they can potentially acquire a retail asset at a knockdown price and add significant value.

Co-living

Co-living is a relatively modern form of communal living where residents get a private bedroom in a furnished home with shared common areas. Now you might be thinking, 'hold on a moment, that sounds a bit like an HMO to me', and up to a point, you'd be right. However, HMOs are just one type of communal living, and the new breed of co-living spaces can differ quite substantially from your typical house of multiple occupation.

The main difference lies in the standard of the communal areas and the underlying concept, which is to build a community. Where HMOs are usually a compromise – most tenants would rather have their own flat but can't afford to rent or buy one – co-living spaces are designed to be a community where tenants want to live together. As such, the quality of the communal facilities is usually of a much higher standard than your average HMO, where communal areas tend to be more utilitarian. In many cases, the landlord actively manages the properties to foster a sense of community, rather than the more hands-off approach of most HMO landlords.

Not surprisingly, the co-living market attracts a younger audience, and the most popular locations are in city centres. For most of us north of 35, the thought of living communally is anathema, however for the young (and young at heart), the solution has a lot to offer. A sense of community with better facilities, a private room, and a city centre location. It's like being a student but without the institutional décor, cheap beer, and relentless spag bol. ☺

It's anticipated that co-living spaces will provide greater investment returns than traditional HMOs in the future. So, there's an opportunity for smaller developers to either build these units to rent or to work with an established co-living provider who will purchase the units once built. Again, there's no need for these to be huge-scale developments; there will still be many opportunities for the small-scale developer.

A word about new build

We're conscious that we've not said anything about new builds in this section, so it's worth putting things into context. The underlying need for new housing means that the demand will be there irrespective of whether you convert an existing property or build a new one. In this chapter, we've focused on where a specific opportunity has come about due to the 'perfect storm'. There's no reason why you couldn't build some office pods (for example) from scratch, as the net result would be the same as if you'd converted an existing building. The problem is that it's riskier and lengthier to build new rather than convert. Which begs the question 'why would you bother?'.

Many people like the idea of new build because they're working with a blank canvas. They can build what they like without the confines of working with an existing structure. But new build has its challenges:

- It generally takes longer to complete a new build project than a conversion project
- You always need planning permission for new builds, whereas many conversions have permitted development rights. As we'll see, the planning system is time-consuming, frustrating, and unpredictable
- With new builds, you must go into the ground, i.e., dig foundations. Because you can't see what's in the ground until you start digging it up, you have a real risk of encountering additional costs (e.g., a requirement for deeper foundations or rerouting pipes and cables) or delays (e.g., waiting for bat surveys or finding archaeological remains).

For these reasons, we always recommend to first-time developers that their first project either has planning permission already agreed or has permitted development rights. In reality, the latter is usually a far better proposition since if a plot or building already has planning permission, it means that the vendor has already priced in the uplift in value. You have a far better chance of retaining that uplift yourself with permitted development.

Summary

Hopefully, this chapter has given you a flavour of the opportunities for small-scale property developers in the current climate. Property will always attract those looking for wealth creation since it's a tangible asset with strong demand and proven equity growth. Becoming a buy-to-let landlord used to be the easier decision, but now it's anything but thanks to increased taxation and regulation. Small-scale property development is fast becoming the de facto choice for those looking to make money from property. The ability to earn significant six-figure profits from small projects in relatively short time-frames is hugely attractive, as is the fact that so much of the work is outsourced to a team of established professionals whose services can easily be acquired by a new developer.

Let's now take a closer look at the tool that can make life for those looking to do smaller developments a lot easier; permitted development rights.

8. The Planning System

What we'll be covering

The planning system in this country is complex, with many intricacies. The good news is that, as a developer, you're not required to become a planning expert who knows every last nook and cranny of the system. Instead, you'll be hiring the services of a planning consultant who will be able to advise you. However, it's such a critical area that you will need to know a reasonable amount, both about the pitfalls of the planning system, as well as its advantages and opportunities. This will ensure that you avoid looking at deals that could take years to get through planning and instead focus on ones where you can move quickly with more certainty, and with luck, spot opportunities that other developers have missed.

In this chapter, we'll avoid doing a deeper dive into the nuts and bolts of the system and its rules but will instead focus on the principles of planning, the risks you'll want to avoid, and the opportunities that currently exist for new developers.

The planning framework

At the risk of stating the obvious, you aren't allowed to build what you like on any piece of land you happen to own, and for good reason. For many years now, the UK government has deemed it a legal requirement that you obtain planning permission from the local planning authority (LPA) before you either build new or, in many cases, change existing buildings. In this way, they can:

- Protect against over-development
- Avoid inappropriate development, e.g., someone building a heavy industrial unit in the middle of a housing estate
- Avoid new developments adversely impacting neighbouring properties, e.g., overlooking
- Stop homes being built in inappropriate areas, e.g., on land prone to flooding
- Prevent unsightly new buildings detracting from the street scene
- Avoid overloading the local infrastructure or creating danger through the poor location of traffic exits etc.
- Prevent people demolishing or changing historic properties so that the nation's architectural heritage is preserved
- And many more besides

A robust planning system therefore is a good thing for society at large, and, as you can see, many different aspects come under consideration.

The current planning system hasn't changed a great deal since the 1950s, and the process, on paper at least, for making a planning application is simple and effective. The LPA enforces a set of rules which govern what can and can't be built. Most of these rules are the same for every part of the country; however, some will be specific to that LPA. LPAs must put forward a Local Plan for government approval, covering their planning policies and proposals for new development. This is publicly available and should be essential reading for those developing locally.

A developer would typically have their architect or planning consultant make a formal application to the LPA using a prescribed format. Depending on the size of the project, the LPA would then have either 8 or 13 weeks in which to consider the application, after which they will either grant or refuse permission. The LPA reserves the right to ask for further information to determine the application and may also require the applicant to undertake specific surveys to demonstrate whether or not a particular problem exists. If the application is refused, the applicant has a right of appeal, which is reviewed by an independent body to ensure fairness.

On paper, then, a simple but effective system. Unfortunately, on paper is where the good news ends; in practice, it's a total minefield. So why is that?

The problems with planning

Let's start by understanding what impact the planning system can have on you, the developer. Your overarching challenge is that you can't build your project unless you have planning consent. And because no project equals no profit, what you crave is certainty. Imagine buying a plot of land with a view to building some houses, but you had no idea whether planning permission would be granted. You'll not only have to fund the land acquisition but there will also be finance and legal costs associated with the purchase and then further costs in having your architect draw up the plans and submit the planning application. If planning is refused, then not only will you be unable to recoup your planning costs and architect's fees, but you'll also be left with a piece of land that will presumably have decreased in value due to planning being refused, which you now need to sell. And finding a buyer may be difficult given that there is no longer an opportunity to develop the plot. If you were ballsy enough to go ahead and build without FPP, then the LPA will likely get you to knock it down and may also prosecute you. Not a great result and unlikely to win you many friends at the council.

Overall, then, planning permission is a deal-breaker on which a fair amount of time and money will hinge, and you want as much certainty as possible before you apply for it.

Let's now turn to the challenges with the planning system itself as, unfortunately, these only add to the uncertainty:

The system is chronically under-resourced

While, in theory, LPAs should take eight weeks or less to determine an application, most LPAs lack the resources to stay on top of their burgeoning in-trays. However, applications don't automatically get granted or refused once the 8-week deadline has passed (13 weeks for larger developments); instead, they simply stay as applications. You'd think there would be some sort of backlash due to all these deadlines being missed. But cynics argue that LPAs are adept at avoiding such accountability. Instead of letting the deadline sail past, they write to the developer just before the end of the eighth week requesting more information. This effectively resets the clock and puts the ball back in the developer's court. Could they have asked for this information earlier? Who knows; however, it would be naïve to think that this stop-clocking strategy never happens. Does this make planning officers terrible people? Not in the slightest; just humans trying to do the best job they can with a chronic lack of support and resources. But ultimately, it's the planning applicant who suffers the consequences.

There are no old, bold planners anymore

One of planning's biggest challenges is a lack of experienced personnel in LPA planning teams. Back in the day, there would be a healthy hierarchy of senior and junior planners. Senior planners were worth their weight in gold because they had the experience to engage with developers and adopt a more pragmatic approach. They could also guide junior planners, who would then go on to become senior planners. Planning departments work best when their team members work together and have access to experienced personnel. Years of chronic under-resourcing have taken most experienced personnel out of the industry, leaving just the relatively inexperienced personnel working in a toxic environment with an impossible workload. Worse still, the pandemic forced all planning teams to work remotely from home, removing the benefit and comfort of bouncing ideas and decisions around the team quickly. We're left with a fundamental role in the planning process, starved of support, resources, and a workable system. As a result, fewer people aspire to become planning officers, and many that remain are frazzled and disillusioned. The government has plans to overhaul the planning system, which is good news; however, it will take time to fix a system that is so fundamentally broken.

The LPA can request a broad range of additional information

In many cases, the information that the LPA can request from the developer will be in the form of a survey, and the list of survey subjects is not short. They can include architectural surveys, bat surveys, tree surveys, parking surveys, etc., and they each have a cost in both time and money to procure. Again, the principle is a good one – only by undertaking a survey can the LPA ascertain whether a problem exists. But if the survey throws up a problem, it could result in planning permission being refused, and so the developer will have no way of recouping the planning application costs. It's worth noting that some surveys, such as a bat emergence survey, have seasonal restrictions, and you may need to wait several months before the survey can take place.

This is where having a planning consultant on board can pay huge dividends as they can advise on the appropriate planning strategy and the surveys that should be submitted along with your application.

The planning system has not been modernised

The system would be deemed cutting edge if you were somehow able to teleport back to 1950, but in today's money, it's archaic. There has been virtually no digitalisation or use of internet technology. As a result, both the LPAs and developers suffer from the clunkiness of a system that is long overdue an overhaul.

Assessments can be subjective

In theory, planning decisions shouldn't be subjective because LPAs must assess applications against planning policy, which is set in stone. In reality, there are many grey areas where LPAs can simply interpret the rules to their preference. This is because there are so many nuances involved in planning that it's impossible for planning policy to be completely definitive. So, if you submit an application that the LPA doesn't like, they often have the scope to refuse permission by interpreting the rules in their favour.

Planning experts do not determine planning applications

You might think that the LPA would ensure that the people assessing planning applications are suitably qualified to do so. The reality is that most people who sit on planning committees have no formal planning training. How do they determine an application if they are not planning experts? Well, it's not much of a stretch to imagine an element of subjectivity might creep in.

LPAs do not always appear to be pro-development

There's a natural tension between LPAs and developers. The latter will typically look to maximise the value of a plot. As guardians of the system, LPAs are duty-bound to ensure that the local environment and its inhabitants are protected. This can lead to a perception by developers that LPAs are anti-development and look for an excuse to say 'no' rather than 'yes'. Both sides would argue the opposite; however, we've heard enough developers' tales over the years to conclude that there's no smoke without fire.

If this all sounds rather gloomy, then you'd be right. However, help is on hand in the form of two factors that can improve matters dramatically for the developer. The first we've already mentioned, namely that the planning system is about to undergo a generational reformation that will drag it kicking (and probably screaming) into the 21st century. The government has committed to making radical changes to the resourcing and infrastructure and the planning process itself. There have been numerous announcements since 2020 trailblazing the changes, and it's fair to say that a number of these proved to be somewhat controversial, which has led to the government rethinking them. 2022 marks the next phase of the journey where the precise details of these changes should become a lot clearer.

Planning reform is all well and good, but it feels a little like 'jam tomorrow'; we have to wait for the full benefit of the changes to be realised. We mentioned that two factors could help you as a developer side-step planning risk to a large degree. Luckily, the second factor, permitted development rights, are not only extremely helpful, but they're also available right now.

The benefits of permitted development rights

Under the planning system, each building is ascribed a 'use class', which reflects its purpose. For example, a residential property has a use class of C3 which has the title 'Dwelling House', and it encompasses houses, maisonettes, and flats. There are separate classes for other types of residential property, such as houses of multiple occupation (HMOs) and also for the various types of commercial property (see Appendix 1 for a list of the current use classes). If a building owner wants to change a building's use class, they'll need to apply for and be granted planning permission. This prevents them from unilaterally turning their house into a shop, a café, or an industrial sawmill, something that you'd imagine their neighbours might take issue with. Similarly, one can't turn a commercial property into a house or a block of flats without first gaining planning permission since it involves a change of use.

As we've already mentioned, the government believes that converting disused or unwanted commercial buildings into much-needed residential homes makes a lot of sense. Consequently, they created new PDRs that permit the use class of a building to be changed without the need for full planning permission. In this way, developers are encouraged to convert commercial buildings into homes because much of the planning risk has been removed.

Creating a single PDR to cover all conversion types wasn't appropriate, as there are many different scenarios. Therefore, each type of PDR was allocated a reference code, and to make matters confusing, this reference code was called a 'class'. So, we now have 'use classes', which determine the use of a building, and 'permitted development classes', which determine the scope of what can be converted (clearly, the Department of Housing wasn't planning on writing an easy-to-follow book about property development). For example, the PDR class 'O' covered the conversion of offices (use class B1a) into residential (use class C3). A list of the key PDR classes at the time of writing can be found in Appendix 2, although we'd urge you to check with your LPA or planning consultant to see if there have been any recent changes.

From the outset, it was recognised that there would be situations where it might be inappropriate or undesirable to convert certain buildings, and therefore some form of oversight would be required. Examples of this include:

- Where the building to be converted is in a high flood risk area

- Where there would be an unacceptable level of noise, e.g., when converting an office block sited next to a factory
- Where there is a high level of contamination on the site
- Where transport access to the site by residents could be unsafe
- Where the conversion of a commercial building could result in a significant loss of employment in the area
- Buildings in conservation areas, AONBs, or listed buildings

Therefore, an approval process would need to be set up that allowed the LPA to assess each conversion project. However, the assessment criteria would need to be limited to pre-agreed 'showstopper' events only; otherwise, there would be no real benefit in creating the PDR. This gave rise to the process known as 'prior approval'. Most (but not all) change of use PDRs require the developer to apply for prior approval to the LPA. The LPA must then judge the application ONLY against the pre-agreed criteria set out in that PDR class. The LPA CANNOT assess the application against any other criteria, even where the absence of the PDR would have resulted in a full planning application being refused. Different PDRs have different prior approval criteria, and some have more restrictions than others. Some PDRs also impose a time limit on the LPA to assess an application.

We should also mention that 'date-stamping' can apply to certain PDRs. Date-stamping is when a PDR specifies a minimum and/or maximum age for a building to be eligible for development. This can either be a specific date or a rolling timescale, e.g., two years. Put simply, if your building is younger or older than the date-stamp, then the PDR doesn't apply, and you would need to apply for full planning permission. As the more entrepreneurial reader may have spotted, if there were no date-stamp, it would be possible to build brand-new commercial units in an area where residential planning permission would not have been granted and then immediately convert them into residential using permitted development. But

115

the government has thought of that and headed it off at the pass, so bad luck. ☺

So, we have a way for buildings to be converted into residential homes without the need for full planning permission (FPP). This significantly reduces the planning risk because the change of use is likely to be the most contentious element of any planning application. Note that while residential conversions are the most popular type of conversion due to the premium that new homes attract, some PDRs also allow for the conversion from one commercial use class to another.

One final point; PDRs do not apply in Scotland, Wales, and Northern Ireland. These devolved administrations have their own planning administrations, and while some rights are specific to each country, none have the scope of the PDRs that apply in England. Please check the respective local authorities and ministries in those countries for full details of the prevailing planning policies.

The introduction of National Space Standards

Homes built subject to full planning permission (FPP) must comply with something called National Space Standards. These standards determine several minimum thresholds for various qualitative values relating to new homes, including the minimum floor space based on the number of inhabitants. For example, the minimum size of a one-bedroom flat for one person with a shower room is $37m^2$ ($39m^2$ with a bathroom). Before 6th April 2021, National Space Standards didn't apply to PDRs, so there were no minimum requirements regarding the size of the apartments that one could build. This created a significant advantage for PDR schemes as it allowed developers to build smaller flats and therefore fit more units into a site, which made it more profitable for them.

On paper, this sounds like it would be an obvious recipe for poor quality housing, yet the reality is that flats smaller than $37m^2$ are far from unfit for habitation. Anyone who has visited a 30m^2 apartment will testify that while small, they are certainly not cramped. Also, as high street lenders do not typically give mortgages on flats that are less than 30m^2, it meant that most developers didn't build flats that were smaller than this since it severely narrowed their target market. The other advantage that these smaller apartments had was that they were more affordable and allowed more people to get onto the housing ladder.

However, every industry has its chancers, and property development is no exception. Cue the arrival of the 16m^2 flat without windows; perfectly legal from a PDR perspective but morally bankrupt on most other levels. Are there people prepared to live in tiny apartments without natural light? Well, we suspect it depends on what their alternatives are. Still, not surprisingly, these rabbit hutches got hammered by the media, and many people got it into their heads that PDRs were a bad thing because they created poor housing.

Luckily there was a solution at hand, namely the mandatory application of National Space Standards, and as of April 2021, these became applicable to all PDR schemes going forward. It may take a while for the bad reputation caused by the rabbit hutch developers to be laid to rest, but today's PDR schemes are subject to the same minimum floor sizes and natural light requirements as any other FPP scheme.

Why you may still need planning permission

There is an important point to note about the change of use PDRs, which is that they only allow for the change of use (no surprises there, then). Once prior approval has been granted, you have a building that is now deemed residential. But if you want to change any part of the building's exterior, you will still need to apply for full planning permission to make the changes. These would include any structural changes, any change to the building's footprint or height, any new openings such as doors or windows, any new render or new roofing materials, and so on. So, in short, unless you're going to keep your converted building the same in terms of its exterior appearance, you'll need to apply for FPP.

This is probably the point where you ask why we've been banging on about the benefits of PDRs if we're going to need to apply for FPP in any event. Well, here's the thing; exterior changes are nothing like as contentious from a planning perspective as changing the use of a building. Providing you're not putting in openings that cause overlooking issues for your neighbours or creating a complete eyesore; then the planners are unlikely to object to most elevational and cosmetic changes. Bear in mind that planning applications are assessed against specific criteria, so if your new windows meet those criteria, then your application will be approved. The LPA can't refuse permission just because they don't like you or your permitted development project.

Don't forget your planning consultant

When considering any development project, you'll be viewing it strategically well in advance. And when it comes to planning risk, you want to close out as many intangibles as possible, and that means hiring the services of a planning consultant. These people can often work miracles when it comes to what they can get through the planning system. They'll certainly be able to advise you on the best planning strategy and tell you what is and isn't possible under permitted development, both in general and with a specific project.

You'll also want to know that any elevational changes like doors or windows will sail through planning, and your planning consultant will be able to tell you this. Most importantly, they'll let you know this before you've purchased the site, so you can be aware of any blockers before committing to the project.

They'll also be able to advise whether it would be better to apply for the change of use via prior approval <u>before</u> you've applied for planning permission for the elevational changes or <u>afterward</u>. For example, let's say you wanted to convert a light industrial building and were looking to put in a few more windows and change the roof to make it look a bit more residential. You would have three basic planning options:

- apply for prior approval for the change of use first and then apply for planning permission to make the elevational changes afterward, once the building is deemed residential
- apply for planning permission to make the elevational changes first (while the building is still light industrial) and then apply for prior approval for the change of use once the FPP has been granted
- Apply for both at the same time

There's no right answer to this as it will depend on both the building being converted and the local planning situation. That's why you must get your planning consultant on board to guide you.

The latest permitted development opportunities

In 2015, the government introduced what arguably became the most well-known permitted development right, namely the ability to convert offices into residential (class O). This spawned a huge rise in office conversions across the country. Since then, a whole raft of additional PDRs has been added to the list, but nothing quite prepared us for the government's changes to the planning system in 2020 and 2021.

To understand the scope of the opportunity these PDR changes presented, it's important to give you a little context. Before

September 2020, every commercial property type had its own unique use class. Shops were in a different use class to offices, as were cafés, gyms, light industrial units, clinics, and so on. It meant that if you wanted to turn your shop into a café, for example, you would first need to apply for FPP to change the use. Then in September 2020, the government changed the rules. They created a new 'super' use class called class E, into which they transferred the following building types:

- Offices
- Shops
- Banks
- Cafés
- Restaurants
- Light industrial
- Gyms
- Clinics
- Health Centres
- Children's nurseries
- Indoor Recreational Centres

For the first time, all of these buildings were placed in a single use class. It means that if you wanted to change your gym into a restaurant, or your shop into a café, you had an automatic right to do so since you were no longer changing its use class. All the uses listed are interchangeable; you can now change any one of them to any other use in the same class E without seeking permission.

Then, in January 2021, the government dropped an even bigger bombshell. With effect from August 2021, they would be creating a new PDR called class 'MA' that would allow any property in use class E to be converted to residential via prior approval. Suddenly all the commercial buildings listed above could be converted into residential without full planning permission.

As class 'MA' is subject to prior approval, there are several requirements, the main ones being:

- The building must be vacant for at least three months prior to the application being submitted
- It must have been in a class E use for at least two years
- It cannot be a listed building or scheduled monument
- It cannot be in an AONB or SSSI
- You will need to carry out any highways, contamination, flood, and noise impact assessments deemed necessary by the LPA
- The building's cumulative floor space to be converted must be 1,500m^2 or less

As PDRs go, these restrictions are relatively benign and shouldn't be a deal-breaker for most opportunities.

The scale of opportunity that this relatively recent change has made is hugely significant. As you can imagine, a substantial number of properties fall into use class E, and for the reasons stated previously, the bulk of these opportunities will not appeal to larger developers. The government is actively encouraging new SME developers to enter the market because it's the only way many existing brownfield sites will get re-developed.

The key PDRs

Appendix 2 lists the key PDRs at the time of writing; however, it's worth calling out what, in our opinion, represent the most attractive opportunities, particularly for the new or inexperienced developer. You should also check with your planning consultant to see if any PDRs have been added or changed in the interim.

Class 'MA' is the stand-out PDR simply because of the sheer breadth of properties in scope, the relative ease with which you can convert them, and the lack of onerous prior approval restrictions. Yes, you can only apply once the property has been empty for three months, and clearly, this won't be an issue for unoccupied premises. But even if the property is tenanted, reaching a point where the 3-month vacancy threshold has been achieved is likely to be manageable for most projects.

Office conversions

These have been hugely popular since the class 'O' PDR arrived in 2015. Offices convert relatively easily to flats because the doors and windows are typically in the right place already, plus the exterior of the building often doesn't require substantial cosmetic changes. There's usually parking on site and the location can be either in or near a town centre or at least next to good transport links. The downside is that the market has caught up with the demand, so office owners and their agents price their stock accordingly. Since offices now fall into use class E, they are subject to the class 'MA' PDR, so class 'O' has been superseded. A little-recognised benefit is that the date stamp for class 'O' was March 2013; however, the latest changes have resulted in the date stamp moving to September 2020, giving us over seven years more stock to target.

Retail conversions

These have become increasingly popular recently, and as we mentioned earlier, they play a crucial role in bringing life back to our new-look high streets. We're talking about turning shops into apartments, whether converting the entire building or just the upper storeys (known as the 'uppers'). Several things have conspired to create a big opportunity for retail conversions. We've already mentioned that the out-of-town retail parks and supermarkets, followed by the internet, drove traffic away from town centres, and thus resulted in less demand for high street stores. Then there's the arrival of the 'just-in-time' supply chain model, which meant that many retailers no longer needed to store as much inventory on the upper storeys of their shops and would instead order in stock on demand. This meant that uppers ceased to be an essential storage requirement for retail, which meant one could convert them to residential without making the store underneath unviable.

One of our favourite PDRs is class 'G' which allows you to put up to two flats above a shop (and any other building now in use class 'E' as well). The space to be converted into flats must be above the commercial element and be connected to it, and you're not allowed to convert the shop itself to residential. Why is this a favourite PDR of ours? Well, it shows how, with a little planning knowledge, you can achieve some quite remarkable things. Let's use an example to demonstrate:

Damien has his eye on a high street store that is currently empty, following the retailer going bust. The building has three storeys, with retail on the ground floor and storage on the two upper floors. The shop is also quite wide, spanning two high street 'units'. Using PDR class 'G', Damien knows he can put two flats in the uppers; however, because of the size of the shop, these two flats would be enormous and therefore wouldn't give him a very good return, compared to, say, building eight one-bed apartments instead (which would require FPP). However, once Damien owns the shop, nothing prevents him from dividing the retail space into as many separate shops as he likes. If he divides it into four individual retail units, PDR class 'G' will allow him to put two flats above each one, creating eight flats in total. This is possible because:

- you don't need planning permission to sub-divide shops
- there is no date-stamp on PDR class 'G', so it can apply to shops that were created yesterday
- there is no minimum size for a shop. In our example, Damien's taken a single shop then divided it into four, but in

theory, he could create 32 tiny shops and build 64 flats above.

- PDR class 'G' applies in conservation areas and to listed buildings, so there are very few restrictions, albeit you will still require prior approval

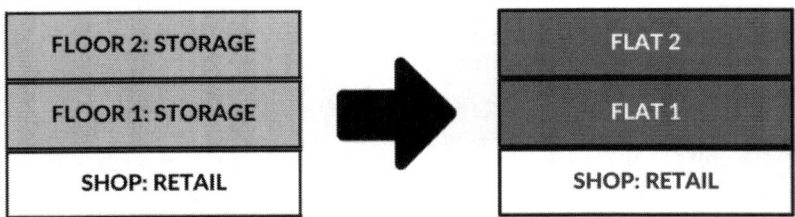

Table 1a: *Damien has a PDR to convert the uppers into two flats, however they would be huge. To create more, smaller flats would require planning permission.*

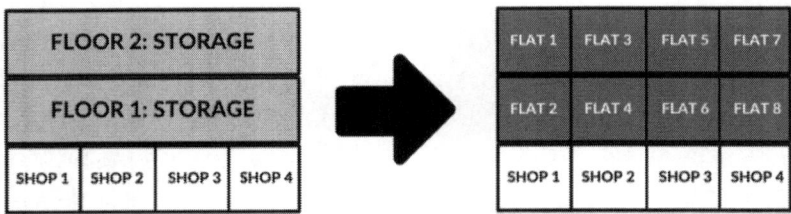

Table 1b: *By first subdividing the shop into four separate retail units, Damien can now put two flats above each WITHOUT planning permission, creating eight flats.*

You can see that with a modicum of creativity, PDR class 'G' has quite some potential. But it doesn't end there. Damien knows that shops now fall under super-use class E, and providing the building has been a shop (or another class E use) for at least two years, he can use PDR class 'MA' to convert the ground floor retail space into residential too. This would give him another four flats, making 12 in total. And if he was required under PDR class 'MA' to keep the ground floor shop fronts as retail, he could look to put flats to the rear of the ground floor by simply reducing the depth of the shops at the front. He would just need to make sure that he exercises the PDR class 'G' option first and the PDR class 'MA' option second.

Suddenly, Damien has an exciting opportunity on his hands. And if he had to retain the four not-very-wide-and-not-very-deep shops, who would want to own or rent them? Well, there's an increasing number of retailers looking for smaller stores. Businesses such as nail bars, vape stores, newsagents, etc., don't need a great deal of space. Alternatively, a company could simply acquire two or more of the shops and knock down the adjoining wall to create a bigger shop.

This ability to combine two or more PDRs is a great example of how huge opportunities can open up with a little knowledge and imagination. It's also why your planning consultant is likely to be on your Christmas card list. ☺

Light industrial conversions

These are some of our favourite PDR opportunities; in fact, we wrote a book all about how to do them (search for "Industrial to Residential Conversions" on Amazon). Light industrial is the term given to industrial units in residential areas. They used to use class B1(c) before being reclassified within the new super use class E. Between September 2017 and September 2020, they had their own PDR called class PA; but this then lapsed. However, from August 2021, these buildings can once again be converted under PDR class 'MA'.

There is a long list of benefits of doing light industrial conversion projects:

- There is little competition; most developers tend to prefer office or shop conversions as they find it easier to envisage the end product

- As a result, there's less likelihood that vendors will have built in a development uplift
- Most developers don't know the tricks of doing these types of conversions successfully
- You're usually able to build directly off the slab, so there are no footings to dig and, therefore, no nasty underground surprises lying in wait
- You'll be working indoors most of the time, so no weather delays (your contractor will love you)
- Most light industrial buildings are effectively large open spaces with walls and a roof, so you have a great deal of design flexibility in terms of layout
- Any contamination is likely to be contained under the existing base. If you're not digging into the base, then chances are the contamination can simply stay where it is
- There are no demolition costs
- You can re-use the existing structure, effectively building a second 'skin' inside the existing frame
- You can often create more interesting living spaces, particularly if you're making a feature of the building's industrial heritage

Bank conversions

It won't have escaped your notice that there are fewer banks on the high street than there used to be, and this trend looks set to continue as we move towards a cashless world with online banking the norm. You'll recall that PDR classes 'MA' and 'G' allow us to convert banks to residential. Many banks were constructed to a high specification; not only did they need to be robust (for security reasons), but they also needed to look attractive and to stand out from the competition. As a result, they can make beautiful apartments, albeit you may find you have the added 'benefit' of a secure strongroom or vault, which may not convert readily to accommodation, but which could provide much-needed storage space.

Office pods

Converting commercial buildings into residential is an obvious choice since the latter commands a premium over most other uses. However, there's nothing to stop you from repurposing or upgrading an existing commercial building for a new commercial use, particularly given the breadth of building types caught under use class E. This can be particularly attractive in areas where residential isn't a great fit, perhaps because there are no other homes locally. One area that has seen a lot of interest recently is the office pod market. Office pods are small office units typically accommodated within a block of similar units. The pods may be completely self-contained or have shared facilities such as toilets, kitchens, break-out areas, and meeting rooms. Pods can either be rented or sold, either to individuals or operators.

The fallback position

This is a little-known but potentially potent tool that can allow LPAs to grant full planning permission where ordinarily they would refuse it. The principle is rooted in common sense, and we'll use an example to demonstrate it. Let's assume that you have an agricultural building e.g. a barn that you're looking to convert to five residential units under PDR class 'Q'. If you meet all the other prior approval criteria, then there's nothing the LPA can do to stop you (PDRs are 'rights' after all). The thing is, PDR class 'Q' would require you to create five terraced units, which does not lend itself to the character of the local area and which may prove difficult to sell. A far better solution would be to create five new detached houses albeit within the same overall footprint of the existing agricultural building, each with its own garden space. However, you don't have a PDR that allows you to do that, so you would need to apply for

FPP, which could, of course, be refused. However, because your proposal to build new rather than convert is demonstrably a better one as far as the local community is concerned, then you can ask the LPA to consider granting FPP as a fallback position. In other words, because you have a right to do one thing, but another option is better from a public interest perspective, then the LPA is effectively obliged to consider granting you FPP for the better option.

While the fallback position is an established legal principle, it's certainly not 'route one', and as a result, the timelines involved in proving your case are likely to be longer. However, it can be a very powerful tool, and the trick is to adopt a collaborative approach with the LPA. Once you've set the scene, take the trouble to find out the LPA's concerns and see if you can accommodate them. This approach is usually far more productive than taking an aggressive stance and trying to railroad the LPA into a fallback decision.

Things to watch out for

One of the biggest tips we can give any new developer is to clear a corner of their desk specifically to house something called the Too Difficult Pile. At face value, this tip doesn't sound particularly insightful, yet it's the lack of one that can cause developers to waste a lot of time at best, and a lot of money at worst, on projects that won't go anywhere.

The problem is that every deal has its good points, and we can spend a lot of time focusing on these and not enough time looking at the bad bits. We can all too readily visualise the stunning duplex apartments we'd build and the substantial profits we'd pocket. But for some reason, we choose to temporarily ignore some of the practicalities or planning challenges until we're a lot further down the line. And by then, we've invested time (and possibly money) which is now potentially wasted. If only we'd taken a reality check at the start, taken off the rose-tinted specs, and put those troublesome deals in the Too Difficult Pile.

So, in this section, we want to mark your card about projects that you should think twice about, even if they sound quite appealing in theory.

Beware PDRs with subjective strings attached

You'll have gathered that the prior approval process requires developers to satisfy various criteria and that these criteria can vary from PDR to PDR. Ideally, you want black and white criteria, so it will be self-evident when you have met them BEFORE you apply for prior approval. However, some PDRs contain prior approval criteria where the benchmark is NOT definitive and require the LPA to assess them. As soon as you rely on the LPAs subjective opinion, they effectively become your judge and jury. You could argue that their assessment is unreasonable, but you're going to have less traction than where it is 100% clear that you have satisfied the criteria.

Beware of untried and untested PDRs

When a new PDR comes into force, there will always be a bedding-in period where LPAs assess applications for the first time. Ideally, you don't want to be in this first wave of early adopters as there could be some fallout from LPAs looking to thwart applications or some other unintended consequence. Bear in mind that the LPAs don't devise PDRs, and so they will be trying to work out how to approach new PDRs as soon as one is announced. It's usually better to make an application knowing that others have already successfully gained approval and any kinks have been ironed out.

Pubs

We recommend that you don't try and convert pubs, despite these being one of the most common types of conversion we get asked about. Their appeal is obvious; they're often attractive buildings that are readily convertible, have parking, good transport links, and are usually in residential locations. However, there are issues. The first problem is that they now fall into a use class called Sui Generis. This is effectively a catch-all for buildings that don't fall into any other category, and as such, there are no PDRs in place. Anything with a Sui Generis use class will require full planning permission, and as we've mentioned, that's not likely to be the easiest or quickest road for you to travel down.

What makes pubs even more challenging is that they're often deemed to be a community asset, one that has been dwindling in recent years. Even though failed pubs presumably couldn't attract enough customers to stay in business, you can expect a strong reaction from both the local community and the LPA if you try and convert one into housing. After all, an empty pub still has the potential to get back on its feet, but that potential disappears forever once it has been converted. There will be far easier opportunities out there, so we advocate giving pubs a wide berth.

Contamination

Contamination typically occurs where a site has been subject to industrial processes or chemical storage and can be prevalent in properties such as industrial buildings and disused petrol stations. The critical point to note about contamination is that liability attaches to the owner of the building, not the business or individual who caused the contamination. As a result, if you buy a property and decide to dig up the foundations, which then causes contamination to affect a neighbouring property or get into the water system, you'll have a potentially colossal clean-up bill on your hands.

That said, historic contamination should not generally be an issue providing you're not going into the ground. Typically, contamination in an industrial building will be locked beneath its concrete base. But if you can build directly off the base, then not only do you not need to dig any footings but there is also no need to disturb any contamination. This ability to build straight off the existing base is one of the attractions of converting industrial buildings. At the end of the day, contaminated soil must exist somewhere; digging it up and moving it elsewhere doesn't eradicate the contamination, and the process of moving it actually creates a hazard.

One final word of warning; never buy a disused petrol station or a site on which a petrol station once stood. The risk of contamination remains high even when the underground storage tanks have been filled in, and you'll have no idea as to the extent of any historic leakage. You have been warned!

Airspace rights

In planning parlance, 'airspace' is the empty space that sits immediately above an existing building, and several PDRs allow you to add additional storeys. For example, PDR class 'AA' will enable you to add additional residential storeys onto an existing detached commercial unit, subject to various minimum requirements and height restrictions. This sounds great in principle, but you must get your structural engineer and architect to guide you on the logistics of adding the additional storeys and the structural integrity of the host building. It's very easy to envisage adding a couple of new storeys, but it can be quite a different issue when it comes to the logistics. You'll want to know precisely how challenging it will be and the likely cost implications before you spend a lot of time on it.

In a recent High Court case, the judge established that the list of criteria that projects must meet for airspace rights was not exhaustive. In other words, you must meet the criteria listed in the PDR, but the LPA could then add to these any additional criteria that it saw fit. This effectively gives the LPA the power to overturn any application since it can simply make up criteria that sinks the application. Ridiculous and unintended, yes. But a harsh reality nonetheless, and one that makes airspace rights a PDR to avoid in our book (and another reason if you needed one for hiring a good planning consultant).

Plots or projects that already have planning permission

We mentioned earlier that for your first project, you should avoid tackling anything that:

a) doesn't have permitted development rights or
b) doesn't have full planning permission already granted.

This enables you to remove a substantial element of risk straight out of the blocks. However, there's a big financial problem with b) (projects where you're buying an asset with planning permission already in place), namely that the vendor has already priced in the value created by having the planning permission in place. Let's explain this in detail because it's a common mistake.

When you see a building plot with planning permission (along with the architect's drawings and perhaps an attractive artist's impression of the end result), who do you think is going to win it? If you were to build what has already been designed, then you're not adding any additional value. So, you will only win it if you're either able to build it more cheaply than anyone else or accept less profit. You won't be able to achieve the former (unless you've got your numbers wrong) and you shouldn't accept the latter.

But what if you've seen a way of adding additional value that the vendor hasn't spotted? Perhaps they've got FPP for two-bed homes, whereas you think you could make them three-bedders. There are two things to think about here. Firstly, it's conceivable that the vendor already tried to get three-bed units but wasn't allowed to or didn't think they'd be approved (you can check their planning application on the planning portal). However, even if they've genuinely missed it, you would still need to apply for planning permission to change the application from two-beds to three-beds. So, you're back to square one, buying a property with no permitted development rights that still requires planning permission.

So, in summary, we highly recommend your first project is a permitted development one!

Article 4 areas

Article 4 relates to restrictions put in place by local authorities that prevent certain PDRs from being exercised. Article 4 directions (as they are known) apply at a local planning authority (LPA) level, so you will need to check the relevant LPA's website to see if any are in place. Most Article 4 directions have been enacted to curb the number of HMOs in a specific area or to reduce the number of office-to-residential conversions. It's also worth double checking the situation locally with your planning consultant.

Planning summary

We've covered quite a lot of ground on the planning side of things, but it's for a very good reason. Planning is one of the critical areas of risk in development, but it's also one of the biggest areas of opportunity. Investing time in understanding the rules and, in particular, the opportunities presented by PDRs will give you a huge advantage over your competition, as will making sure that you have a good planning consultant on board. The good news is that you don't need to know more than every other developer in the country; you only need to be able to spot an edge that the relatively small number of people who look at any given development opportunity haven't spotted. A development opportunity is worth different amounts to different people. If you can sweat the asset better than your competitors, then you can afford to pay more than they can to acquire it and are therefore much more likely to secure the deal.

Your competitors

It's worth adding a final word or two about your competition. You might have presumed that a newbie developer is going to be on the back foot, coming into a market where there are many experienced players already operating. The reality is that newly-trained developers are on the <u>front</u> foot, and that's because they've invested time and energy in understanding where the best opportunities lie.

Many experienced developers aren't interested in understanding the latest permitted development rights. This is because they know what they know, and so they keep on doing it. They stick to their knitting. After all, if you're making good money doing new-builds with planning permission, why would you try and do something else? So, don't make the mistake of assuming that every existing developer knows more than you do about the latest opportunities, as many won't.

Another key consideration is that most developers operating at the small-scale end of the market have a finite capacity for projects. For example, if you found three cracking deals when you were looking for your first one, you're probably not going to be buying all three. Instead, you'd pick the best one and pass on the other two. It follows that when a deal comes onto the market, not everyone will be looking at it, or will have the capacity to take it on.

We've now reached the end of Part 2 of the book, which we hope gave you a perspective on the large number of current small-scale development opportunities out there. The vast range of properties that we can now convert under permitted development coupled with changes to our work patterns and office requirements have created a new and unique opportunity for developers. For those that can gain an edge by maximising the value in such buildings, the future looks very bright indeed.

Ok, it's now time for us to head to Part 3. Most people don't have a problem getting their heads around the fact that property development can make you rich. Their bigger challenge is believing that they could tackle a development project on their own without any previous experience.

So, let's turn our attention to HOW you can go about becoming a first-time, small-scale developer, even if you've zero experience in the world of property up to now.

Part 3

How Do I Become
A Property Developer?

.

9. How Can I Get Credibility?

A highly leveraged model

One of the biggest mindset blockers that any new developer encounters is their perceived lack of credibility. They think, who on earth will lend me money, sell me a project or work with me if I've never developed property before? By the end of this chapter, you'll see that it's perfectly possible to create enough credibility to develop property, whatever your level of experience.

As we mentioned earlier, property development is a highly leveraged business model. As the developer, you're not required to draw any plans, lay any bricks, or understand the load-bearing capacity of existing foundations. You will have a team of professionals working for you who will know all this stuff; in the preceding examples, an architect, a main contractor, and a structural engineer. You can recruit these professionals very easily because their business model involves them being hired by property developers for a fee. In fact, property developers make up the lion's share of their client base. And they're not hidden from view; simply google the term 'architect' or 'structural engineer', and you'll see a whole list of them to choose from.

Here's another perspective for you to consider. Imagine that you wanted to build an extension on your home. Would you be worried that you'd have to learn how to design and build one yourself? No, you'd simply find some local architects and builders, assess which of them could do the best job at the right price, and then hire them to build it for you. You'd oversee the project, and when the architect asks you where you'd like the windows and which skirting board design you prefer, you'd be required to make a decision. You may also be required to make cups of tea (five sugars, please) and lay on a few custard creams. But all of the technical stuff and the heavy lifting are done by other people. Your job is to tell the team what you want and then pay their bills, being on hand to answer any questions they may have along the way.

In some respects, developing a property for profit is no different from building a home extension. The project won't happen unless you instigate it, and you'll need to appoint a team of professionals to do the work. You'll also need to make decisions along the way and arrange the necessary finance to ensure everyone gets paid. And you won't have to make as many cups of tea, which is a bonus.

Hopefully, you can see that far from cutting a sad and rather underwhelming figure in this cast of characters; as a new developer, you're the central protagonist. You're the entrepreneur who's pulling a team together to take advantage of a property development opportunity. Without you, nothing would get built, and no one would get paid. You're playing the lead role, and as we'll go on to discuss, you're already very well qualified to do it.

You are the future

Another common question we get asked is why would anyone in the industry want to work with a newbie developer? Surely, professionals and lenders would much rather do business with someone who's got a proven track record?

The answer is that, in many respects, they probably would. But imagine if everyone in the development world only worked with experienced developers; ultimately, they'd run out of clients after all the existing developers had retired or died out. So, every part of the development industry NEEDS new developers to enter the market because they will become the experienced developers of the future. They know that a developer who does one project successfully is very likely to go on to do many more, and so they have the prospect of a long-term relationship with you. The future of the industry is in your hands – so no pressure ☺.

Perhaps the easiest way of getting to grips with those 'could I really become a property developer' doubts is to think of it the same way you might think of becoming a buy-to-let landlord. Could you do it? Well, thousands of ordinary people have done it before you, and the business model is 100% proven. Do you need to learn some new skills before you jump in? Absolutely, but these aren't highly technical or difficult to understand. You effectively play the role of the Chief Executive Officer or CEO; you're the person that calls the shots, but you don't do the heavy lifting. Just like a landlord, you'll need to find a property at a reasonable price, make sure the numbers stack up, secure the finance and appoint a team to get the property generating money. So, if you think you could be a landlord, you should think about being a developer. In fact, many of our students combine the two roles, a very profitable combination, as we've already discussed.

But we know what you're thinking; yes, it's a highly leveraged role, and yes, you're probably more than capable of becoming a property development CEO. But there's still a lack of anything tangible. You may have some lofty property development aspirations, but currently, not much else.

What you need is a brand.

The power of branding

When most people think of a brand, they think of a business in the public eye. Companies such as Apple, Coca-Cola, and McDonald's all spring to mind as stellar brands known the world over. But what does a brand say about a business? Come to think of it, what exactly is a brand? It all seems a little bit intangible.

We've heard many definitions of 'brand', but one we keep coming back to is a very simple one:

"A brand is a promise."

In other words, when you interact with any business, their brand is giving you an expectation (or promise) of what you will receive or what your experience will be. As a property developer, your personal and business brands are very much connected. However, it's important to note that they're not the same.

One of the key differences between your brand and Coca-Cola's is the importance of personal values. When you interact with the Coca-Cola brand (e.g., buy a can of Coke), the values of the company's CEO are not at the forefront of your mind. You're not sure you know who the CEO of Coca-Cola is, let alone what their values are. Your decision is based almost entirely on the product itself.

However, when someone interacts with you as the CEO of a small-scale property development business, your personal values will be both highly transparent as well as critical to your success. Here are some examples of the people you will be engaging with:

- *Commercial lenders:* these people will typically be lending you six-figure sums
- *Private investors:* they will be lending you their own money and will need to be confident they'll get their money back
- *Estate Agents:* they will be getting paid a commission if you buy from them, but only if you complete on the sale
- *Professionals:* They will be getting a significant four or five-figure fee from you

As you can see, these are not inconsequential relationships for the people involved. There's a significant amount of money at stake, and it links directly to these people's livelihoods. As a result, these people are going to be scrutinising you very closely. It's vital then that what they see looks confidence-inspiring and highly professional.

Now, you may be thinking that you'll be absolutely fine. After all, over the years you've had hundreds of meetings with all sorts of people, and you always come across very professionally. In fact, you're a real 'people person'. Unfortunately, that won't be enough to convince them on its own; you'll also need a brand to back you up.

Perception is reality

Human nature requires us to be judgmental to survive. In our cave-dwelling days, misjudging a person or situation could lead to physical harm or even death. As a result, our subconscious mind, whose primary objective is to keep us alive, would interpret every scrap of available information to determine whether there was any danger. Back then, we didn't have the luxury of seeing how things panned out before deciding whether something would kill us. Consequently, we would form a judgement almost instantly, and that judgement would mature as events unfolded.

While things have certainly evolved since then, we're still very adept at making snap judgements, and we'll make them routinely in every situation. Consider a scenario where you meet someone for the first time. Even if your meeting is limited to only a quick handshake and exchange of pleasantries, you will still pass judgement on them. You will decide whether the person is trustworthy and honest or someone you should be wary of. Perhaps there's something not quite right, even if you can't say precisely what it is. It's just a gut feeling. Well, your gut feel is your subconscious telling you to be wary, and you dismiss it at your peril.

Humans are naturally egocentric, so we tend to overestimate our own importance. But this is good news when it comes to gaining credibility as a new developer.

When we consider becoming a new developer, our mindset is often excitement combined with anxiety and fear. Excitement because we're entering a new and exciting world that could prove life-changing. And fear and anxiety because we've never done it before. We tend to worry that our lack of experience will be completely transparent. Surely everyone we speak to will smile knowingly and think, "look at that newbie developer".

Become credible FIRST

You only get one chance to make a first impression, and in property development, you want to make a good one. A common mistake that many new developers make is putting the cart before the horse (and many don't realise they even <u>need</u> a horse). They can't wait to meet lots of agents and go on lots of viewings, so they do precisely that. Or they go out and try to recruit their professional team. But they do it before they've created a brand (if we had a 'buries head in hands in exasperation' emoji, we'd use it here).

This is a massive own goal. Let's use commercial estate agents as an example to explain why. Estate agents of any description only require a buyer to have two critical things. The first is an offer that is acceptable to the vendor, and the second is to be proceedable. This proceedability requirement is vital. There's no point in an agent recommending that an offer be accepted, no matter how good it is, if the buyer looks flaky or unprofessional. That's because there's a high chance that the deal will fall through at a later date. And if this happens, no one is happy. The vendor is unhappy because their sale has been delayed. And the agent is furious because they've done a load of work with no fee to show for it yet, and they've now got to start marketing the property all over again. The buyer in such circumstances is often persona non grata for obvious reasons, and we'll leave you to speculate on how enthusiastic that agent will be to receive any future offers from them.

Imagine that an agent has received an offer on a property from two brand new developers, Sam and Alex. Sam rocked up unannounced on the way back from Sainsbury's in jeans and a T-shirt, having seen the site in the agent's window. He had no business card, but that was because he didn't have a business, and there was certainly no website for the agent to look at. Sam didn't have an elevator pitch and couldn't describe what he wanted. However, he seemed very enthusiastic about this particular property and said he was keen to give development a go.

On the other hand, Alex had her virtual assistant make an appointment to see the agent and turned up looking very professional, albeit in a business-casual sort of way. She handed over a nice-looking business card with a professionally designed logo across the top and talked eloquently and concisely about what it was her business did and what she was looking for. When the agent checked out Alex's website, they were impressed; it was well-laid out and professional-looking, plus it had details of some of the professionals on her team (the agent even recognised one of them, a prominent local architect).

So, assuming all other things are equal and they both offered the same amount for the property, which offer do you think the agent will be recommending that their client accept?

Some developers never work out that they need to operate like Alex and are likely to sit at the bottom of the pile. Others start out like Sam and then build their brand later. The thing is, the agent's first and lasting impression is the one that will shape their opinion. The answer, then, is to get your brand sorted BEFORE you meet any agents.

Avoid the 'blagging' minefield

One of the holes that new developers can often fall into is the blagging minefield. This is where they get asked a question that relates to their depth of experience (or some similar attribute) and they respond with either with a slight exaggeration, a minor porky-pie or even a gigantic whopper. You DO NOT need to do this. Your professional team have more than enough experience of building homes and will be very capable of delivering your projects. You do not need try and make up stuff to make you sound more experienced than you actually are.

The reality is that you inevitably get found out, and then people start wondering what else doesn't quite ring true. Given the importance of your relationships with the people you'll be talking to, you simply cannot afford to have them doubt your authenticity, so please don't start them wondering by exaggerating any aspect of what you do, or what you've done.

Who would want to do business with YOU?

Because we're all human, we each have the usual quirks and hang-ups that plague our inner thoughts, which can often prove to be highly counterproductive. One of the more unhelpful moments is the feeling of insecurity we can get when we're operating outside of our comfort zone. In development, this can often manifest itself when dealing with other people. When we start, everyone we deal with has more experience in development than we have. We worry that we might look stupid, and that people may not want to do business with us because of our lack of experience.

If this is you, let us give you some words of reassurance. Hopefully, this short story may help (don't worry, it's shorter than the last one ☺):

You may have seen in the news a while back that Richard Branson has a new(ish) cruise line venture on the go called Virgin Voyages. As far as we know, Mr. Branson had never started a cruise line business before, so we presume he must have gone out and hired a whole range of people from the industry to procure all the expertise he needed for his new company. There would be experts on administration, technical advisors, IT, guest services, logistics, HR, entertainment, ticketing, engineering, legal and compliance, and probably dozens of other departments besides.

We suspect he didn't hire all of these people personally but instead employed a Managing Director who could oversee all of the day-to-day stuff. These people had decades working in the cruise line industry, yet poor old Richard was still wearing his 'L' plates. He had the idea and entrepreneurial spirit to make it happen. But he knew so little about running cruise lines; surely he must have been very much on the back foot...?

Roll forwards to the inaugural board meeting of Virgin Voyages. Consider how nervous Richard must have been feeling immediately before he entered that boardroom, about to be confronted with a sea of experts. And there he was, still wet behind the ears but supposedly the man in charge. What would happen if he got asked an easy question and didn't know the answer? He'd look foolish in front of the entire team! What an earth was he thinking? Surely, he's way out of his depth?

Now, we need to make a small disclaimer here – we admit we weren't invited to the Virgin Voyages inaugural Board meeting (nor any of the subsequent ones come to mention it), so we can't say for certain what happened. However, we're pretty sure that if there <u>were</u> some nervous people at that meeting, we suspect that Mr. B wasn't one of them.

Hopefully, instead of nodding sagely in agreement at our story, you'll be shaking your head in disbelief. Of course, Richard Branson wasn't nervous! He's Richard Branson, billionaire entrepreneur, adventurer, and prospective space explorer. He's started dozens of businesses and created the hugely successful Virgin brand. He's one of the most recognisable and respected businesspeople in the world. So, we suspect that pretty much everyone else at that inaugural board meeting would have been more nervous than him. Was anyone really going to ask him how many cabins there are on the Queen Mary, which way is starboard, or whether Duran Duran are available to do a summer season? Not at all. And in any event, we expect he'd been well-briefed by his Managing Director before the meeting and so wouldn't be going in completely clueless.

There's not much subtlety in our analogy, so hopefully, you can relate your role as the CEO of your new development business to Richard's role as the CEO of Virgin Voyages. And perhaps your Project Manager would be the equivalent of Richard's Managing Director. Ok, the scale of your business is several thousand times smaller, your project is far less ambitious, and we suspect there's less swimwear involved. But ultimately, it's the same role. None of the people on your professional team would be getting paid unless you had started your business and made this project happen. No one expects you to know the inside out of property development because they know you're not an industry professional. You're an entrepreneur bringing a team of experts together to take advantage of a great business opportunity. And you ARE the head honcho.

So, when you engage with people as the CEO of your business, it's essential to think of yourself as Richard Branson (or any other successful entrepreneur that you admire). If you get asked a question you don't know the answer to, say you'll have one of your team look into it. Yes, you're the most important person on the team because, without you, nothing would happen. So, believe it and act like it, because that's precisely what you are.

Well, we were getting quite emotional towards the end, but hopefully, that paints a picture of the mindset you need to have as you go into any business venture that sits outside your comfort zone. And on the subject of building your team, it's high time we looked at how you can surround yourself with this cast of high-quality experts who will be delivering your development project.

It's time to recruit your professionals.

Ian Child & Ritchie Clapson

10. How Can I Build A Great Professional Team?

Property developers don't build houses.

Now, that may seem a bizarre thing to say, since if there weren't any property developers, then surely no houses would get built at all? But what we mean is that developers don't physically build houses. They don't lay a single brick; they don't create the drawings; they don't advise on planning. And very often they don't even manage their projects. In fact, virtually all the work involved in building a house (or converting a commercial or light industrial building) is done by other people. So, while property developers don't do that much, they are still responsible for houses being built.

So, who is this team of professionals that do all the work?

Well, here is a list of the people that typically get involved in a property development project, whether it's a new build or a conversion:

1. Architect
2. Planning Consultant
3. Mechanical & Electrical Engineer
4. Structural Engineer
5. Residential Estate Agent
6. Commercial Estate Agent
7. Project Manager

8. Cost Consultant
9. Commercial Finance Broker
10. Commercial Lender
11. Private Investor(s)
12. Contractor
13. Interior Designer
14. Solicitor
15. Accountant
16. Tax Advisor
17. Asbestos Advisor
18. Warranty Company
19. Insurer
20. Health & Safety Consultant
21. Lighting Specialist
22. Landscaping Specialist

and potentially several others, depending on the project.

All these professionals have several things in common (none of which will surprise you):

1. They work for an agreed fee (as opposed to taking a slice of whatever profit the developer makes)
2. They will have appropriate qualifications and many years' experience in their area of expertise
3. They are available to hire by anyone (yes, even first-time developers)
4. They are all appointed either directly or indirectly by the developer to work on a specific project

If you've been exposed to the property training industry for any length of time, you'll have come across a phenomenon known as a 'power team'. What is a power team when it's at home? Well, it's a group of professionals that the property entrepreneur has pulled together to work on their behalf. This power team can exist in both the landlord model and the development space, and at face value, there's nothing terrible about the concept whatsoever. Ok, the name has a bit of a Marvel Comics twang to it, but at the end of the day, it's just a group of professionals who a property entrepreneur uses in their business. For example, a developer's power team would include their architect, accountant, project manager, structural engineer, planning consultant, and so on.

However, you need to be a little wary since the power team concept isn't a perfect solution. The problem arises because most people start not knowing what roles they need in their power team, let alone who would be the best people to appoint or how to go about finding them. So, if an enterprising property trainer comes along and promises students direct access to that trainer's own power team, then it can seem like a massive shortcut. After all, the students now have a ready-made team to support them without lifting a finger. And not just any old team; it's the very same team that their super-successful property trainer uses. What a stroke of luck!

Unfortunately, it may not be as helpful as you might think. The first problem is a logistical one. Our own preferred Project Manager and Contractor are based in Hampshire, while our favourite architect specialises in commercial conversions. So, if you were doing new build projects in Yorkshire, at least three members of our power team won't be much use to you.

The other major drawback with the power team access thing is that you don't have a relationship. We've built up a friendship with our professional team, which in many cases goes back several decades. We've done multiple projects with them and suffered many highs and lows together. They know that we're good people to work with and that we deliver repeat business for them. Imagine if we referred every person we trained to our own team; how important would those referred people be to them? The answer is not very important at all. They'd be just one of hundreds of names.

Luckily the answer to the problem is straightforward; you need to go out and build your own power team. Of course, this could include people from someone else's power team, as long as you make sure that they're going to be relevant to what you're doing and that you forge your own relationship with them. And, in this chapter, we'll teach you how to go about it.

The business model for professionals

First, let's establish a few facts. The first is that all your professionals, without exception, will get paid a fee for their work. It might be an hourly rate or a fixed price. But either way, their remuneration is going to be fee-based. This is crucial since the alternative would be for your professionals to take some sort of profit share from your project, and with all due respect, this isn't going to be hugely attractive for them. What if you turn out to be a complete duffer? Or what if you never complete the project or can't sell the finished units? If there's no profit, they won't get paid, so it's far safer for them to charge a fee instead. That way, they get paid no matter what happens to the project and no matter how savvy you turn out to be as a developer.

Why would they want to work with you?

Another critical question that would-be developers often ask is why would people want to work with them? After all, brand new developers have zero development experience, and presumably, professionals would much rather work with clients who already have development projects under their belt.

One of the unfortunate aspects of being a property developer is that the role doesn't automatically come with the blessing of immortality (or curse, depending on how things are going for you).

As a result, these allegedly highly-prized experienced developers have a habit of retiring at some point and ultimately dying out. This means that unless your professional team members want to run out of clients, they're going to need to find some new property developers to take their place. These will then become their experienced property developers of the future. That will be you, then.

The commercial reality is that a developer who does their first project successfully is very likely to go on and do further projects. From your professional team's perspective, this is excellent news because it can mean multiple fees from the same client over time. Of course, there's no guarantee that every new developer will be successful, but given that they'll still get paid even if a developer is rubbish, they're on to something of a win-win. That said, some new developers can look like a better bet than others, which is why we explained the importance of branding in the previous chapter. This makes you look good in front of everybody, including your professional team.

It's also worth remembering that these professionals only get paid by property developers. In this context, we're using the term developer in its broadest sense, but the point is that there isn't another group of people that give them business. An architect designs buildings for people who are developing property. So, as a new developer, you're very much in the driving seat when it comes to hiring professionals. Hopefully, that's put your mind at rest.

The power of referrals

So, where do you find these professionals, and how can you tell a good professional from a bad one? The backstop could involve you scanning through the online Yellow Pages (or Google, if the Yellow Pages reference leaves you scratching your head in youthful bemusement). But simply sticking pins in the phone book or clicking the first entry on your search engine isn't going to guarantee a good pick. What you really need are recommendations.

Most new developers don't know many professionals. And quite often, the ones they do know aren't always that useful. For example, we once worked with the owner of an old industrial building and converted it into residential apartments. However, before we did the deal, the owner had looked to see what could be done with the site. As he already knew an architect, he got them to develop some designs for which he was charged a five-figure fee. However, the plans were for luxury apartments which weren't a great fit for the property's location, which, being polite, wasn't exactly Belgravia. The problem was that the owner's architect friend specialised in high-end residential developments. And because he wasn't given any specific brief, he just came up with a high-end design by default. In the end, we used a different architect who specialised in conversions. We built basic entry-level flats using permitted development, which were completed more quickly and for a lot less cost. So, not all architects, contractors, accountants, etc., are created equal; you need to appoint someone with the relevant experience and skills in the type of development you're looking to do.

So, going back to the point about getting recommendations, you'll be wanting to get people to recommend professionals to you. For sure, you can start by having a good old google to pull together a list of potential candidates for each discipline, but after you've interviewed people, be sure to ask for their recommendations for other team members. Clearly, you won't be asking a Project Manager to recommend other PMs; however, there's no harm in asking them to recommend Architects, Contractors, Structural Engineers, etc., and vice versa. If you make this a discipline every time you meet a professional, then you'll quickly build up a picture of who's good and who's not.

The recruitment process

While each member of your team is an important appointment, you're not getting married to them, and there's no shame in ditching poor performers ahead of project number two. That said, changing professionals mid-project can be problematic, so it pays dividends to make sure your team is as duffer-free as possible from the outset.

So how can you achieve this?

The trick with finalising your professional team appointments is to be thorough. It can be very easy when relying on recommendations to simply take other people's word for the quality of a firm or individual. The reality is that a business can deliver a 5-star experience for one person and a 1-star experience for another - check out reviews on Amazon or TripAdvisor if you want to see how polarised people's experiences can be.

While recommendations are a great starting point, you'll want to create a checklist for every potential team member. You should check the obvious things, including:

- The size and scale of their business
- Whether they have experience in your type of project
- References from both current and past customers
- Whether you can pay a visit to a current site
- Who you'll be dealing with day to day on their side
- Rates, fees, and terms
- Contracting arrangements

You should also bear in mind that your commercial lenders will be particularly interested in your professional team, so they'll be kicking their tyres pretty hard too. One tip we like to give students is to make sure that as a client, you're neither too large to be their main thing nor too small that they don't jump to attention when you shout for support. The sweet spot is arguably to represent about 20% of their revenues. That way, they have more financial stability than if you were their only client, but you still have enough clout to call the shots when you need to. Companies House will give you a steer on the size of their business, assuming they're a limited company or LLP.

Here are some more top tips to help you with your recruitment:

- Make sure that you have a B list handy for each discipline just in case. Good people are always in demand, and there's no guarantee that your contractor or PM will be available when your project happens to come along.
- If you've interviewed five architects, then document who would be your second choice if your first choice wasn't available. Don't rely on remembering your thought processes later down the line.
- Face-to-face meetings on their home patch are the best approach for interviewing professionals, as you can see their body language and gauge the size and 'feel' of their operation.
- Make sure you know who your day-to-day contact will be, as it might be someone you've not yet met. If so, be sure to get an introduction before you commit.

Since you'll typically be pulling your team together before you have a project for them to work on, you're not going to be signing any contracts at this stage. What you're doing instead is appointing people as 'preferred partners' of your business so that they know they'll be your first-choice partner when your first project arrives.

One tip that can pay dividends is to avoid creating a clique within your team. This can occur when everybody has a track record of working with each other, and they all get on famously. On paper, this sounds like a positive, but the reality can turn out to be expensive. Imagine if the contractor makes an error, and the project manager fails to call them out on it. It will just go down as a cost to the project, and you'll end up paying for it as a result, which isn't fair. The best answer lies in ensuring that you have a blend of people on the team, some that may have worked together before and some that haven't. You certainly want your project manager to ask tough questions and tell tales out of school if someone has screwed up.

Recruiting a Non-Executive Advisor (NEA)

You may be aware of a role in corporate life known as a non-executive director (NED). These are people with expertise, contacts, and experience who can advise the executive board of a business. While they don't play a role in the company's day-to-day operations, they attend regular Board meetings and lend their expertise to matters and strategic decisions. A key aspect of their value lies in their experience and ability to offer alternate views and solutions to the business.

A concept that we advocate at propertyCEO is acquiring a Non-Executive Advisor when doing your first development project. Like a NED in some respects, your NEA will have a great deal of experience in the construction/property development sector (we're talking 20+ years) and are likely to have worked either as a developer or in a professional capacity, e.g., as an architect, project manager, etc.

An NEA will provide you with four key benefits:

Contacts

They will know people in the industry and be able to make recommendations and facilitate warm introductions.

Credibility

Having an experienced NEA on board gives you kudos and provides a lot of confidence, particularly to commercial lenders. A key concern that applies to any new developer is their lack of experience, and it's very reassuring to know that a new developer has a seasoned pro on the team who can help ensure that no mistakes are made.

Advice

Your NEA will advise you and bring the weight of their knowledge and experience to bear. Sometimes there might be a bump in the road; more often, it might be simply another perspective from someone with way more experience than you. Either way, the ability to have someone advising you on your role as CEO can be invaluable.

Deals

While this isn't the primary objective of having an NEA, there's nothing to stop them from becoming a funnel for your deals. You'd be surprised at the number of deals that reach the desks of experienced pros, and there's no harm in asking them to keep an ear to the ground on your behalf.

It's important to note that, unlike a NED, the role of NEA has NO legal responsibility to you or your company other than what you might include in your agreement with them. This is an important point since most people will not be familiar with the NEA role and might assume in error that, like a NED, it carries some statutory obligations to your business.

Why would someone agree to become your NEA? There are several reasons:

Payment

First and probably foremost, you're going to be paying them for their trouble. Considering that these people sit at the top of their tree professionally, it will need to be a significant sum to make them interested. Typically, it would be a five-figure sum that could pay for a nice family holiday or a new car, although the exact amount will be influenced by the size of the project and how much interaction you expect to have with them.

It's not a massive amount of work for the NEA

Most of the value that NEAs bring to the party is already a sunk cost for them, yet for you, they are benefits that money simply can't buy. For example, their contacts list could be invaluable to you, yet it costs nothing for them to share it. The same goes for the credibility they bring to your business. In fact, the only actual cost to them is their time. They'll want to be confident that you're not going to be a burden, so you'll need to be clear upfront exactly how much of their time you expect to take up. Typically, this might be a fortnightly 60-minute phone call plus any ad hoc calls should an issue arise. Their biggest concern is likely to be that you don't know your backside from your elbow as a developer and so will be calling them every five minutes with a daft question. Getting your branding sorted in advance will undoubtedly be a big help here, since it will ensure you already look like a complete professional.

Most people enjoy helping others

We're all teachers at heart, and we've all experienced the pleasure of passing on our knowledge at one time or another to people who have less experience than we do. Once the NEA is comfortable that they're receiving fair compensation for their efforts, most will relish the prospect of helping you and adding value. After all, it's not as if they have to write reports or crunch numbers – they're simply giving you their verbal thoughts and advice.

The role of NEA is not an industry-defined role in development, so you will have to go out of your way to find someone suitable. The trick is to try and find someone for whom the money is a secondary consideration. Ideally, you want someone whose primary goal is to help you succeed; the fact that they get paid well for their troubles is a bonus.

We recommend that NEAs get remunerated through a share of the project's profits after you've sold your units. In that way, their fortunes are entirely aligned with your own. Paying a monthly consultancy fee doesn't work so well since they're getting paid before you are. You want them to be there for you at the end of the project, particularly if there are any eleventh-hour issues to contend with.

So, that's the recruitment process covered at a high level. You really shouldn't worry about whether people will want to work with you. Remember, you're the boss who pays their fees. If you find anyone does look down their nose at you, then move right along; there are plenty more fish in the sea. You certainly may find that your project may be too small for some businesses, but that's not a problem; there will be plenty of others happy to come on board.

Let's now turn our attention to one of the most significant areas of concern for most new developers, which is where exactly am I going to get all the money I need to make all this happen?

11. How Will I Raise All The Money I Need?

Finding the money to undertake development projects is often perceived as the biggest challenge by many new developers. They often assume that they'll need a small fortune in the bank to fund their deals from the outset and don't know how much money it takes to become a developer. Let's start by offering you a brief and entirely pain-free mind shift, which is this; you need to be thinking of money as a tool rather than an asset.

Let us explain what we mean. You're going to be hiring an architect to design your project because you don't know how to design buildings yourself. The same goes for every member of your professional team; you hire them either because they can do something you can't do (or maybe you CAN do it, but you don't WANT to). And in return for this work, you'll be paying them a fee for their trouble. You should think of money in the same way. If you don't have any cash or have some money but choose not to use it, you'll have to 'hire' (borrow) some money and pay a fee to a commercial lender or some private investors for the privilege. Money is simply a tool to do a job. When you need an architect, you hire one; you don't enrol in college to try and become one. The same applies to money.

Does this mean that you can take on multi-million-pound developments without any of your own cash? Technically, yes;

however, some commercial lenders will demand that the developer has some skin in the game, and we'll be covering this later in the chapter.

But first, let's start by understanding exactly where the money will be coming from. You've already had an insight into this area from our story involving Tom and Vicki earlier, but let this serve as both a refresher, plus we'll be putting some more meat on the bones.

The structure of property development finance

The conventional funding arrangements for buying your own home (or, for that matter, a buy-to-let property) involve getting a mortgage from a bank or building society. You buy the building for an agreed price, and the bank will fund the purchase. Usually, the mortgage will be for a figure of less than 100% of the property's sale value because the bank wants you to put in a deposit. The size of this deposit can vary, but its purpose is to give the bank some protection. It means that, should you default on your mortgage repayments, the bank can (quickly) sell the property for less than you paid for it and still get all their money back.

Development finance works slightly differently, albeit you'll be very relieved to know the lender still has a significant amount of protection ☺. To avoid confusion, we're going to call the organisations that provide funding for development projects 'commercial lenders' instead of banks, although technically, many are banks, albeit not of the high street variety.

The first difference is that two loans are involved in property development rather than one. The first loan is known as asset finance. This is the money lent to the developer to fund the purchase of the land to be built on or the building to be converted (the 'asset'). The commercial lender will usually be prepared to finance up to 70% of the asset purchase price, which means you'll need to put in a deposit of the remaining 30%. This deposit can either come from your own funds or you can borrow it from private investors.

Let's say we were to buy an office building for £200k that we're planning to convert into flats. We would expect our commercial lender to lend us £140k, leaving us to fund the remaining £60k either personally or through private investors. If we compare this to purchasing a buy-to-let property where the bank will typically want a 25% deposit, we can see that the loan to value proportions are not too dissimilar. However, the big advantage with development is that you can borrow the deposit from private investors, whereas in most situations, your buy-to-let deposit would most likely be funded entirely by yourself.

The second loan you'll need is called development finance, and this is the money that will pay for the cost of turning your plot of land into a house or your old office building into new apartments. There are two bits of good news attached to obtaining the development finance. Firstly, it will be provided by the same commercial lender that agreed to lend you the asset loan; you won't need to go and find someone else. The second piece of good news is that you won't have to put down a deposit; the commercial lender will advance you 100% of the development finance amount.

If we go back to our £200k office conversion example and assume that the development cost is £300k, then the financing would look like this:

- You or your private investors: £60k
- Commercial lender (asset purchase):   £140k
- Commercial lender (development finance): £300k

You may be thinking that it's nice of your commercial lender to advance you 100% of the development finance without asking you for a deposit. However, it's not quite as generous as a first glance might suggest. The first thing to appreciate is that every pound you spend on developing your project will add to its value. So, if the lender needed to step in and sell the property halfway through, its value will have already increased due to the development funds that have already been spent.

The second noteworthy point is that the development funding doesn't magically materialise in your bank account in its entirety on Day 1. A standing joke in commercial funding circles is that the only thing to arrive on-site if a lender advances 100% of the development finance upfront is the developer's new Porsche. Lenders want assurance that the project will progress to completion with all the money they've lent being invested in the project. The way they do this is to release the funding in several tranches in arrears. So, before receiving your first tranche of funding, a surveyor will need to visit your site and ensure that an amount equal to this payment has already been spent/accounted for. For example, if their first tranche payment was £50k, then the surveyor will expect to see that the site reflects an expenditure of £50k's worth of labour and materials or thereabouts and will report back to the lender accordingly. If all they can see is an empty field and your shiny new 911, then you may be waiting a while for your first tranche payment to get signed off ☺.

This tranche funding does raise another critical consideration for you as the developer, namely ensuring you're on top of your project's cash flow. You'll be paying bills from your contractor and your team of professionals during the development, and you'll be relying on your development finance to draw down the funds to settle these. What happens if there's a kink in the financial hose because the surveyor isn't happy that a payment can be drawn down? In that case, you'll need to make sure that you either have enough funds available to cover these bills until the draw down payment is received or that you can get your creditors to agree to wait. Not an insurmountable problem, but you wouldn't be the first developer to have been caught out by a lack of cash flow on a project that could have ultimately gone on to make a lot of money.

We'll talk about how you can obtain both commercial finance and private investment in a moment, but first, it's important to understand the way you should structure your property business.

Setting up your property development business the right way

How you structure your business is so critical we appoint each of our mentees with a personal Business Coach to help them get it right. Why is it so crucial? It's because if you get it wrong, you can end up spending a small fortune in tax that you didn't need to. Given that the sums involved in small-scale development are usually meaningful, it's a subject that's worth getting right first time.

The other challenge is timing since the taxman is not known for allowing people to fix things retrospectively. If you finish your development and then suddenly realise that you could have saved £80k in tax if you'd set things up differently, the Inland Revenue is unlikely to allow you to unpick everything, turn back the clock and start again. This, unfortunately, was the exact position that one of our students faced when they first came to us. It's great that they now know, but a real pity they hadn't done their homework beforehand. So, do your learning before you start and not as you go.

We need to add an important disclaimer here: we're not qualified to give you financial or tax advice. Also, everyone's situation is different, so giving (or taking) generic tax or business structuring advice is rarely a great idea. We highly recommend that you seek the advice of your accountant or tax advisor before setting out your stall in this area. Feel free to share the ideas and concepts in this chapter with them, but ultimately, they should be the ones to advise you on the best corporate structure and tax arrangements for your personal circumstances.

Understanding Special Purpose Vehicles (SPVs)

The first thing to say about business structures is that for each development project you undertake you should set up a brand-new limited company. Known as a special purpose vehicle or 'SPV', this is the legal entity where all contracts and transactions occur. You, together with your joint venture partners, if you have any, will be directors of the SPV, and it's the SPV that will have the loan agreements with the commercial lender. The SPV will also own the land or property you intend to develop and will be the entity that your professional team members will contract with and get paid by.

Commercial lenders always insist that developers start a brand new company (SPV) for each new project because it utilises a legal framework and a well-defined set of established responsibilities. There's also no baggage attached to a new SPV; no prior trading or other directors who could muddy the waters. Re-using an existing SPV company is rarely acceptable for the same reasons.

The SPV is not part of your brand as such, and there's no requirement for you to overthink your naming conventions. For example, it could be called 24 Acacia Avenue Limited or ABC Developments Project Number 1 Limited.

Another key benefit of having a separate SPV for every project is risk mitigation. If one of your projects were to experience an issue, then the liability does not extend outside the SPV. Conversely, if you were to operate all of your projects within a single limited company, then a problem on project three could impact the entire company, including your other projects.

The holding company concept

Another concept that can be particularly tax-efficient for property developers is the creation of a holding company. This is a limited company owned by you (and possibly other adult members of your family) that holds the beneficial interest in each SPV. When your project is completed, the units sold off, and your commercial lenders and private investors repaid, what you should be left with is a healthy profit sitting in your SPV. If you own the shares in the SPV, then the profit will come to you personally, which in turn means that you'll need to pay personal income tax on it. Your income tax bill will be based on <u>when</u> you received the profit and could potentially push you into a higher income tax bracket for that tax year, which may not be ideal. By having the SPV owned by your holding company, the profits are instead passed up to the holding company and will stay there until you wish to take them. This gives you a range of options:

- You could defer taking some or all of the profit to max out your personal income tax allowances
- You could direct some of the profit to a spouse or other family member who is a shareholder of the holding company to maximise their tax allowances
- You could reinvest the profits in your subsequent development. Typically routing profits from SPV1 to the holding company and then reinvesting them in SPV2 will be more tax-efficient than taking the SPV1 profits personally and reinvesting in SPV2

Some, but not all, of our students already have businesses. Some may be related to property (for example, a limited company that owns their buy-to-let portfolio), while others relate to their 'day job'. Either way, it is usually possible to incorporate these businesses within the holding company structure outlined above.

Again, you should discuss this with your accountant or tax consultant.

Your brand is not necessarily a company

We talked earlier about creating your brand. This is the name that your development business is known as e.g. ABC Developments. It's important to note that this brand does NOT need to be set up as a limited company. There's no problem if you DO set it up as a company, there's just no requirement to do so. The reason for this is that all your transactions and contracts on a project will need to go through an SPV. As a result, there will not normally be a requirement for you to have a second, separate limited company; your brand can simply be a name and a website. This should save you a few hundred pounds a year, since there's an admin cost to running a company, even if it's just the cost of your accountant filing the annual return.

Why would anyone lend you money?

This is a frequent question from those new to development, and it's not an unreasonable one. After all, the sums involved will typically run to five, six, or maybe even seven figures. And if you're a brand-new developer, who on earth is going to have enough faith to lend you that sort of money, whether they're a commercial lender or a private investor?

The answer lies partly in you having the right perspective. New developers tend to overestimate the importance of funding, and as a result, they tend to think that lenders and investors hold all the cards. That's not to say that the funding isn't critical; it's simply one of the ingredients needed to bake the development cake.

It's like the man pulled up on the side of the road because he's run out of petrol. He needs to get to his destination and so the most important thing in his world is finding someone with fuel. This can be the approach taken by novice property developers looking for private investors. Yet a few miles up the road, there's a petrol station owner who desperately wants to go somewhere, but she doesn't have a car. Her perspective on what is the most important thing is completely different.

So, before we assess what IS the most important thing, let's take a reality check on where our friends in finance are at. Banks currently pay a miserable interest rate, so no investor will be looking there for a healthy return. Stocks and shares can produce good returns, but they can also be volatile. On the other hand, property has always been perceived as a good investment asset. After all, there's a reason your bank will lend you money to buy property, but it won't lend you the same money to invest in the stock market.

Here's a couple of facts for you to consider; your commercial lender will typically charge you between 5-10% interest plus fees, while your private investors will typically receive 8-10% interest from you. If we compare that to the other investment opportunities available to these people and organisations, your proposition is highly compelling. Better still, because the underlying asset is property, it can't realistically lose its value in the same way that stocks or shares can. In other words, there aren't too many places where investors can get such an excellent level of return with relatively low risk. As a result, if you've got a good project, then you WILL be able to find finance. After all, there's a lot more money looking for a 10% return than there are 10%-returning deals looking for money.

There are two other perspective changes that you may also need to make. The first is that borrowing money from commercial lenders is not the same as obtaining a home mortgage. When you buy your home, your mortgage company will first ensure that what you're paying for the property isn't over the odds. But the second and most important thing they'll do is check that you have the means to repay them. That's more or less it. But with commercial lending, you, as an individual, are not nearly as important. The number one thing the bank will be interested in is the deal itself. If the deal is great, then the fact that it's a new developer's project is not usually a showstopper. The second thing they'll be interested in is your team. After all, these are the people who will physically do the work. How experienced are your contractor, your architect, and your project manager? Have they worked on similar types of projects before and at the same scale? And how robust are they financially? Then, and only then, will they look at you, the developer. After all, if there's a great deal being built by a great team, the developer's credentials, while important, are not likely to turn it into a bad deal. That said, you still need to approach lenders and investors in the right way, which is one of the critical skills we teach our students.

The second perspective change goes back to the principle that old developers eventually die out. While the banks may like every developer to have lots of experience, the reality is that unless lenders embrace the developers of the future, then their own businesses will run out of customers. As a result, the lending market will always have a solution for new developers since they secure its long-term future. And as we will shortly see, they do an admirable job of de-risking their positions.

Commercial lending options

Commercial lending is the most common route for developers to go down, and since they'll be lending you up to 70% of the asset finance and 100% of the development finance, you can see that they play an important role.

Traditional commercial lenders are not your typical high street banks but lenders who specialise in niche investments such as property development. Some have multiple specialisms, while others are dedicated to property. Some operate as traditional banks while others are family offices, companies that manage the investments of the very wealthy.

Peer-to-peer lending (a.k.a. crowdfunding) has also become a popular choice for developers looking for finance and is now an attractive alternative to the traditional solution offered by the commercial lenders. Crowdfunding organisations effectively play the role of a broker by finding investors (both individuals and corporations) and introducing them to development opportunities. They have the expertise to critique both the developer and the deal, so their investors have confidence that the investment opportunities on offer have been vetted. The investor ultimately makes their own decision as to whether to invest and takes the associated risk. Crowd funders also look to offer a more developer-centric experience than their commercial lending counterparts, yet they will have similar criteria for developer credibility and deal profitability.

There are also many angel investors; high net worth individuals who invest professionally in property developments, new business start-ups, etc. They tend to have sophisticated criteria and processes for approving funding, just like commercial lenders and crowd funders, albeit they may have greater flexibility since there is ultimately a single decision-maker.

One overarching observation about commercial lending, in general, is that lenders like to take minimal risk. Not only will they demand a first charge on the asset, but they'll also demand you sign a Personal Guarantee (more on both of these later). They also have a great deal of flexibility when it comes to pricing. There is a mind-boggling array of charges that can apply to development loans. Quite apart from paying interest, there can be arrangement fees, fees for drawing down each payment, fees for the surveyor to authorise a drawdown, even fees for paying the money back. This can sound like a lot of fees (and it is); however, if your deal stacks up with all these fees and interest included, then your project is still viable.

As a first-time developer, you may find that some of your rates are loaded to account for the additional risk, but this is not a problem if the deal still stacks. Lenders have a wide range of options to mitigate their risk; charging extra fees, higher interest rates, and lower loan-to-value percentages (i.e., a bigger deposit needed) are all in play. However, once you've established a track record, you can usually expect the deals you'll get from lenders to become more competitive.

Your good friend, the broker

You'll have gathered that commercial lenders are quite important in the world of property development since they're lending most of the money. But how do you go about finding one that will work with you? While some lenders 'go direct' most offer their services through a broker network. These commercial brokers will play a critical role in you securing commercial finance, and the good news is, they are on your side. To be clear, brokers operate in the world of the banks; for crowdfunders, you'll need to go direct.

There are a significant number of variables when it comes to organisations lending money on a development project. You (the developer), your financial robustness, your experience (and your team's robustness and experience), the amount of capital you have to invest, the type of development, its scale, its location, and so on. Not all lenders will lend on every project, and it's the broker's job to find you a commercial lender that will be happy to do business with you.

We recommend that you work with at least two or three brokers so that you're getting good access to the entire market, as they won't all be knocking on the same doors. The broker only gets paid when a finance deal goes through, so you know they'll be working hard on your behalf. They'll also be able to advise you on your business CV, the level of analysis you need to produce for each deal, and the pros and cons of any deal from a funding perspective. We've spent a lot of time making sure that our students can present deals in the most professional and confidence-inspiring way, and we give them the templates and analysis tools that our own brokers have approved for them to use. You need to make sure that you do the same, so talk to your brokers to ensure you're getting a good steer on what's required.

Brokers will need you to tell them a lot of information not only about your prospective project and the team you've assembled but also about you, your experience, and your financial situation. It's imperative that you come clean about any skeletons you may have lurking about in closets. If you don't, then you're setting yourself up for a major fall. In these days of financial transparency, it would be naïve to think that skeletons won't be uncovered when a lender does their due diligence on you. Imagine what an idiot you (and your broker) will look when the lender rejects your application because you failed to disclose something you should have. So, the best advice is to get it all out on the table. You may be surprised; what might go down as a black mark on a home mortgage application may be far less critical to a commercial lender. Remember that they're not only looking at you but at the deal and the team as well, so honesty is the best policy. It may narrow your field, but at least your broker knows what they're working with and can find you a solution.

Repaying the interest

A key advantage of property development is that, while you're borrowing a significant amount of money, you don't usually need to make any repayments until the finished units are sold. This is often very appealing to landlords who, in stark contrast, have to start paying interest on their buy-to-let mortgages from the moment the money is borrowed.

Getting paid during the development

One of the challenges with property development is that the profits only materialise at the end. It means that the developer needs to have enough savings or income to put food on the table while the project is ongoing, although you'll likely be developing in your spare time so will have an income from your existing job or business.

In many cases, this may not be a problem. However, one option that some commercial lenders can accommodate is a development management fee (you may remember in our earlier story that both Vicki and her friend Steve were able to earn a £30k development management fee). This fee is paid to you from the development finance during the construction phase and is likely to be a percentage of the construction cost. For example, on a project where the construction costs are £300k, a 10% development management fee would pay you £30k. The fee recognises the role you play in the oversight and management of the project and shouldn't be confused with the (entirely separate) fee that your project manager receives.

It's important to note a couple of things. Firstly, these fees do not increase your net profit from a project; they simply bring a part of your profit forward. In the above example, your £30k fee is a cost to the project, reducing your profit by the same amount. So, if you were planning to make a £200k profit when you sold out, you'll now only make £170k if you take the fee.

Secondly, not every lender is happy to have this arrangement, so you should speak to your broker if you need a fee, so they only target lenders who offer it. Some lenders prefer to let you have your profit at the end since that keeps you focused. More enlightened lenders recognise that giving you a small amount of advance profit ensures you prioritise the project without worrying about paying your bills. Also, the 10% figure is not set in stone, and different lenders will have different criteria.

The two-exit requirement

One thing that you should ALWAYS have as a developer is at least two exits on every project (and your commercial lender will insist that you do). You need to know that if there's a problem with your proposed exit (for example the market tanks or you're struggling to sell the last units), that you have an alternative exit strategy that you can rely on. In practice this usually involves a simple switch. If you were initially planning to sell your units, then an alternative exit would be to rent them out. This would mean switching your finance to a buy-to-let mortgage and paying back the commercial lender who funded the development. You could then rent out the unit(s) until you were able to sell them. Alternatively, if you were building to rent, your alternative strategy may be to sell the units.

Securitisation

We mentioned the concept of a 'first charge' earlier. This is where someone has a charge over an asset, and in the case of property development, the asset is usually the land or building being developed. It means that that you, as the developer, have an obligation to clear the debt first when you sell the asset. In the event of a repayment issue, the charge holder (usually the commercial lender) could sell the asset to repay their loan.

All homeowners who have a mortgage are very familiar with a first charge since their mortgage company will have one on their home. If they fail to make their mortgage repayments, the mortgage company can ultimately repossess their home and sell it to get their money back. They can do this because they have a first charge on the property.

Your commercial lender will typically want a first charge on the building or land you plan to develop. For them, this represents a reasonably safe bet; after all, they've only lent you (up to) 70% of the purchase price, yet they have the first charge on an asset worth 100%. Do you think they'd be able to sell a property for 70% of its value quickly? Of course, they would, which is why it de-risks the deal for them considerably.

It's possible to have a second charge over an asset, although most commercial lenders won't usually allow this. Since the first charge lies with the bank, you won't then be able to offer the same security to your private investors. You can certainly let them have a personal guarantee (a "PG"; we'll cover these shortly), and you could potentially offer up a charge on some other asset you own, such as another property or a business debenture. However, we would argue that additional security outside a PG wouldn't usually be necessary for private investors. After all, it's a question of risk and reward. They're getting an excellent rate of return precisely because there's an element of risk in their investment. If they don't want any risk, they can stick it in the bank and earn a pittance – it's their choice.

You could technically offer a first charge to private investors if there were no commercial lenders involved, and you were sourcing all your finance privately. There are a couple of reasons we wouldn't recommend doing this for your first project. Firstly, your commercial lender will thoroughly analyse your deal inside and out before lending you any money, and this should give you great comfort. If you've made an error in your calculations, then it's more likely to be flushed out. On the other hand, your private investors won't be checking your numbers and, in any event, will expect their loans to be repaid at the end of the project. The project's profitability calculations rest on your shoulders alone (gulp). The second reason for using commercial finance on your first project is that it gives you a track record. Your first project will likely be your simplest, quickest, and smallest. Commercial lenders will be aware that it's your first development and will have weighted the deal to account for that additional risk. However, once you've got a development under your belt, not only do you now have a track record with the lender, but you're also likely to command sharper rates going forward.

Using your own money

At the start of this chapter, we mentioned the concept of doing developments without putting in any of your own money. There are a few considerations here. Firstly, some commercial lenders do not require you to put in any of your own cash. They WILL still need you to pay a deposit, but they're happy for this to be money you've borrowed from private investors. Other commercial lenders insist that some of the private finance you raise comes from you. The required amount will often be a percentage of the project value (i.e., the asset and development costs combined). For example, Vicki's Dillon Street project had an asset cost of £300k and a development cost of £350k, and so the project value was £650k. If her commercial lender had insisted that she put in 2% of the project value personally, it would mean she'd have needed to stump up £13,000 of the £90,000 deposit, with the balance funded by private investors. It's not a king's ransom but a sufficient amount to constitute 'skin in the game'.

Secondly, many seasoned developers choose not to invest in their own projects because of investment diversity. They already have a financial outcome riding on the success of each project, so while providing the investment funding as well would reduce their finance costs, it means that all their eggs are now in one basket. A better risk mitigation strategy would be to invest in a different project or a different asset class altogether.

Always make sure that you ascribe a cost to any money you invest in the project. It can be tempting to think that you're somehow making the project cheaper by investing your own money since you won't be paying interest to a third party. The payback for your investment is that you'll make more profit in the end. However, we strongly recommend that you still pay yourself interest on the amount you put in, just like any other private investor.

Can you do development without putting in any of your own money? Technically this is certainly possible, but we wouldn't say it was the easiest route, and therefore we'd struggle to recommend it. Using none of your own money would mean:

- finding a lender who is happy for you to borrow 100% of the deposit from private investors, and;
- borrowing an additional amount from private investors to cover the additional purchase costs we mentioned earlier, including stamp duty, conveyancing, professional fees, and survey costs.

Also, please remember that you will have further costs in establishing your brand, getting educated in development, and ongoing costs incurred when driving to viewings, networking with people, and other operational expenses. Remember that when you borrow money from a private investor (as opposed to a joint venture partner), you have an obligation to pay them back their capital plus interest at the end of the loan, irrespective of how well your development project has gone. Also, having some working capital gives you greater flexibility should you have any unexpected costs on the journey. So, yes, it's doable, but we'd suggest having some cash of your own is highly desirable.

One final consideration; it would be great to think that your second project will come along the day after you've just pocketed the profits from your first. But if it comes along beforehand and all your cash is already tied up in Project 1, then you might not be able to put in enough of your own money into the second deal in time to secure it if you're working with a lender who requires you to have skin in the game. Just bear in mind that it might be prudent to hold some cash back for this contingency.

Finding private investors

The source of private investment can often come as something of a surprise, particularly to new developers who didn't think they knew anyone who had money and thought that finding investment would be an uphill struggle, as indeed for some it can. On the other hand, some developers already know of people who may want to invest, or they may have their own investment funds available, while others may not know where to start. Let's start then with a few basic facts.

The first interesting fact about private investors is that just about anyone can be one. You can't search for them on Google, and they don't have a name badge, job title, or business card. They could be your mum, your Aunt Flo, your best friend, a work colleague, someone you met down the pub, your accountant, your dentist, or someone you met at a networking event where you mentioned you were a property developer who worked with private investors. The point is that lots of people have money to invest, but it isn't usually their main 'thing'. Some have savings, while others may have cashed in their pensions. So, the good news is there's a vast number of potential investors out there; the bad news is you don't know who they are or what they look like.

It's worth noting that private investors who are <u>not</u> JV partners do not have a say in what happens on the project. They don't have input into decisions; they are simply providing finance. Yes, you will want to keep them updated on the project's progress, but you won't be asking for their input or approval when you choose which type of skirting board to buy.

The significant advantage that you have as a developer is that you can typically offer a private investor an 8% to 10% return on their money. As we've said previously, there aren't too many places serving up those sorts of returns. Better still, you pay this interest once you've sold the units you've built, so you don't have to budget for any repayments during the project term. So, you have an attractive proposition, but there's a problem; you've no track record, and most people won't know you from Adam, so why would they trust you with their money?

Some of the lowest-hanging fruit will undoubtedly be people who know you already, e.g., friends, family, colleagues, and acquaintances. They won't have told you they have money to invest (because people usually don't), but they have the advantage that you're already operating in their circle, and they presumably trust you. They know that if you ran off with their money, you would be leaving an unpleasant brown deposit on your own doorstep, which you're highly unlikely to do. The important thing then is to tell everyone what you do and let on that there are some attractive investment opportunities for your select group of private investors.

The biggest secret to securing private investment is not to ask people for money. This sounds somewhat counter-intuitive, but there's a simple psychology behind it. If you ask for money, people tend to assume a couple of things. Firstly, they'll think you don't have any of your own money to invest (otherwise, why would you be asking to borrow theirs). Secondly, unless they're a blood relative, they'll automatically assume that they weren't the first person you asked to invest. As you're still asking for money, then presumably you didn't get it from all the other people you've asked, which suggests that at least some of them refused to lend to you. If so, surely they should think twice about lending to you too?

The other thing that asking for money does is put all the power in the investor's hands. It makes them the buyer and you the seller, and that's not the way you want things. Instead, you want investors to be falling over themselves to be one of the few that get selected to be part of your exclusive investment network. We're not trying to con people into a dodgy investment here. We're offering an outstanding return on a property-related investment that's based on a wealth creation model that's worked handsomely for centuries. Plus, we're prepared to give a Personal Guarantee, so they'll have significant confidence that they'll get their money back. The question they'll be asking themselves is NOT 'would I like to receive an 8-10% return on my money?', since the answer will almost certainly be 'yes'. No, their question is much more likely to be, 'do I trust this person enough to believe I'll get my loan repaid on time and with the interest they promised?'. Consequently, you need to take your prospective investors on a journey that establishes confidence in you and makes them aware of the risks and processes involved with such an investment.

Getting people to invest with you is all about how you position yourself. Again, it's an area that we focus a great deal on in our training, but in essence, the key is to position your investment opportunity as an exclusive 'club' where membership is by invitation only. You work with a select panel of private investors but are always happy to talk to new investors about future investment opportunities.

Here are a few golden rules that should apply when dealing with private investors:

Less is more when it comes to investors

If you're trying to raise, say, £50k of private investment, you don't want fifty investors lending you £1k apiece. Sometimes the smaller the investment, the louder the noise coming from the investor, and you'll end up having a full-time job trying to keep all your investors happy, in check, and updated. Ideally, you want a handful of investors, and the best way of achieving this is to set a minimum investment level. That way, you can weed out smaller investors at the outset and ensure that you're working with a manageable cohort of more significant players.

Have a Plan B for private angel investors

At the other end of the scale lies the private investor who's prepared to lend you all the money you need. This certainly isn't a bad thing from your perspective; however, it should prompt you to consider what would happen if your investor has a change of heart for whatever reason. They could change their mind, have another use for the money, or fall upon hard times. What would you do then? It's not a reason for not working with them, but make sure you've considered a Plan B. Also, be mindful of the amount of control your investor has. Sometimes a sole investor thinks they're entitled to be a part of the management and decision-making process, so make sure the ground rules are established right from the outset.

Have more investment pledged than you need

Ideally, you want to be recruiting investors before you need their money; otherwise, you'll find yourself up against the clock when trying to get your deals across the line. This means getting decisions in principle from your investors in advance, so you can call on them as and when a deal moves forward. It's easy for investors to say yes in principle, but physically handing over the cash can be a different matter altogether. You may find that some investors get cold feet or suddenly find the funds are not available when you want them. Your solution is simple; make sure you have more investment pledges than you need. That way, if your first-choice investors get flaky, you've got other investors in reserve.

Be clear on communications and input

Some investors are needier than others. Be sure to clarify that a) their investment is passive, and they won't be actively involved in the project, and b) that they will get regular scheduled updates on progress; they're not entitled to call you out of the blue, demanding your attention. This suits most investors very well, but you should set expectations just in case.

Have the investor journey nailed down

Nothing engenders a lack of confidence quicker than when someone offering you an investment opportunity doesn't know all the steps in the investment process, so don't fall into that trap. You should be familiar with every part of the investors' journey and be able to answer any question they might have. Also, it pays dividends to have a draft loan agreement available for potential investors to look at, so they can understand what's involved legally (we'll talk more about these in the next section).

Be upfront about the risks

You have a moral responsibility to ensure that the investments you're offering are a good fit for your investors, which means letting them know upfront about the risks involved. Being proactive rather than reactive on this subject helps inspire confidence. For example, a key risk from the investor's perspective is any delay in completing the project or selling the units. The loan agreement will spell out what happens in this instance; typically, the loan will continue with interest accruing in the usual way, or you may agree to a higher rate. However, your investors need to know that there is no guarantee that you will return their investment on a specific date since, until you've sold your units, you won't have the cash available to repay them.

Get clarity on what's on offer

There are three key things you need to know from your investor:

- how much are they looking to lend;
- how long are they looking to invest for, and;
- when they will be able to start their investment.

People looking for investment opportunities may already have their funds tied up with other investments, or they're planning to invest a future windfall, e.g., a pension drawdown or a bonus from work. You need to establish whether there are any time sensitivities in terms of when they can start investing and if there's a deadline when they want to have an investment in place. After all, they may be happy to invest with you, but they're not going to be earning any interest until the project starts, so may not be prepared to wait indefinitely.

Take it one step at a time

A common failing of many new developers is that they adopt a wham, bam, etc., approach to their relationships. They believe that they only have one shot at the title, and therefore they need to get everything out on the table on Day 1. Statistically, it takes an average of seven touch points before people do business with each other. As a result, the chances of anyone agreeing to invest with you the first time they meet you are extremely remote. Therefore, your goal at the first meeting should be to get another meeting in the diary; no more, no less. This may be the goal of the next few meetings, too. By doing this, you build trust, respect, credibility, and confidence, and consequently, a much greater likelihood that the two of you will end up working together.

Loan agreements

You should have a loan agreement in place with every private investor. It doesn't matter if it's your mum or your best friend who lends you the money; they should still have a loan agreement with you. The reason is simple; if you get knocked down by a bus tomorrow (please try not to), and there's no legally-binding loan agreement in place, how will you (or they) know that they are going to get repaid? Potentially with great difficulty is the answer, unless there's a loan agreement in place.

Loan agreements don't need to be complicated. At their heart is simply the details of the loan; the identity of both parties, the amount being borrowed, the term, interest rate payable, and other related information. This is then wrapped up in the necessary legal words to make it contractually binding before being signed by both parties.

Many websites provide templates for loan agreements, or you can get your solicitor to provide you with one. Whichever route you take, we strongly recommend getting a solicitor to sign off on the final version. Not only can the law change, but you also want to make sure you have some comeback if the contract doesn't deliver what you intended. Using a solicitor gives you both comeback and confidence that the document is fit for purpose.

Understanding the FCA rules

The Financial Conduct Authority (FCA) took over some of the responsibilities of the now-defunct FSA several years ago and is currently responsible for regulating certain aspects of the financial services industry in the UK. Since property development is not a financial service, the FCA doesn't frequently cross the developer's path; however, there is one area where it does, and you must make sure you know their rules and abide by them.

The area in question is that of private investment. As a developer, you're looking to find private investors and enter into loan agreements with them. The FCA affords private investors a level of protection to protect them from disreputable characters who might be looking to charm them into bad investments. While this almost certainly isn't a description of your good self, the FCA doesn't know that and needs to ensure that you abide by a set of rules when engaging with private investors.

We'll describe the main principles of the FCA rules here, but we strongly recommend that you read them for yourself and get your accountant to guide you through them. The law in question is FCA Policy Statement 13/3 (a.k.a. PS 13/3), and you can download a copy from the FCA's website (fca.org.uk).

In plain English, if you want to promote an investment opportunity to a third party where their capital is at risk, you must first ensure that they are either a High Net Worth Individual or a Sophisticated Investor. The FCA sets out the criteria that individuals must meet; however, it's YOUR responsibility to ensure that your investors meet these criteria.

A High Net Worth Individual must have an income of over £100k per annum or assets in excess of £250k over and above their pension fund and equity in their home residence. A Sophisticated Investor must meet one of the following criteria:

- They have been a director of a company with a turnover of at least £1m within the last two years
- They've made more than one investment in an unlisted security in the last two years
- They've been a member of a business angels network for at least six months
- They've worked professionally in the provision of private equity or SME finance in the last two years

Please note that these criteria are subject to change, so please make sure you check PS/13/3 and any FCA updates for the precise wording.

The good news is that a straightforward loan sits outside PS 13/3. Put simply, the law doesn't apply if you're borrowing money for a fixed term and then repaying it with interest, which will be the loan model used by most developers. However, it _will_ apply if you're offering an investment opportunity where the investor receives a share of the profits (or losses), i.e., a joint venture or profit share. The FCA deems this a riskier investment since the investor's capital is at stake. Therefore, it should only be offered to investors who meet the criteria mentioned above.

So, if you're not joint venturing, then you'll sit outside PS 13/3, but if you are, then you'll need to understand your responsibilities.

Types of loan

When it comes to private investors, there are four main types of loan agreement you could enter into:

Option A: Straightforward loan for a specified project

This is the most common loan type, where the loan relates to a specific investment. The interest is rolled up and becomes payable along with the capital at the end of the project.

Option B: Straightforward loan with interest payments

Similar to the above; however, the interest is paid monthly throughout the loan period.

Option C: A fixed-term loan agreement

This is where the loan is for a fixed period, e.g., 5 or 7 years. Typically, such an arrangement will only come into play once you have an established track record with an investor. As the developer, you're able to borrow the funds to use on any project during this period, giving you greater flexibility.

Option D: Profit share loan agreement

This is a joint venture partnership where some element of the investor's return is linked to the level of profits made from the project. You'll need to ensure that your investor meets the FCA's HNWI or Sophisticated Investor criteria.

Our strong recommendation is to stick to Option A for your first project, and indeed there's no harm in sticking to these types of loan for every development you do.

Giving a Personal Guarantee (PG)

Personal Guarantees (also known as PGs) can appear quite scary at first glance, but they're a commitment that all developers need to get their heads around. They're simply part of doing business as a developer. Let's take a look at what's involved.

A PG is a commitment you make to a lender or investor that you will repay them the money they've lent you. Not an unreasonable obligation, but the critical point is that you'll repay their money even if your project fails to make a profit. In this unlikely but possible scenario, it means you'll be repaying them from your other assets if there's not enough profit from your development project to cover it.

This doesn't mean the bank could repossess your house, as they might do if you didn't make mortgage repayments on your home. Ultimately, the lender would take you to court, and the court would determine the terms under which you would have to repay the amount owed. The court could certainly force you to sell your assets, but perhaps it's unlikely that this would include the roof over your head. That said, it's imperative that you understand what's at stake when you sign a PG.

So, on paper, then, PGs are a big commitment. But before you head screaming for the hills, let's put them into perspective. One of the things that commercial lenders are good at is lending money. And one of the things that they're terrible at is building houses. So, if we look at things from their point of view, their worst-case scenario is that you get halfway through the development and then decide that it's all a bit much and decide to throw them the keys before scarpering. They would then be left with a half-completed development and a lot of work to do to try and move the project forward to completion to get their money back. So, to dissuade you from having the thought even enter your head, they insist on a PG as a nuclear deterrent. Does it mean they'll press the button at the drop of a hat? Of course not; it's the last resort. But it will ensure that you, the developer, remain focused on getting your project across the line.

It's worth adding that the lenders in question are all too familiar with the ups and downs of development and are not expecting every project to run like clockwork. They can be sympathetic when challenges occur because, in many cases, they've not got much choice. They can't change the situation, nor do they want to get involved. But they DO want the developer to a) tell them what's happening and b) come up with a solution. Lenders start getting nervous when bad news isn't communicated. Bury your head in the sand, and you may incur their wrath, but a pro-active approach with good communication will usually stand you in good stead.

Another key point to note about PGs is that they usually require you to have joint and several liability. This means that if there is more than one stakeholder (for example, if you have a joint venture partner working with you on the project), then the bank can pursue either of you for the entire debt, even though both of you have signed a PG. If you have greater assets than your business partner, the lender could come after you for the entire debt, even though you technically only owe half of it. It will then be down to you to try and claim back the 50% share from your partner. While this may seem a little inequitable, the reality is that the PG exists to protect the lender, and this joint and several arrangement gives them their best shot at getting their money back. However, it's vital that you consider this point carefully when entering a JV arrangement. Would the lender be more likely to come after you or your JV partner if the worst were to happen?

The lender will usually require you to have the PG document inspected by an independent solicitor and signed in their presence. That way, the lender is assured that an independent legal professional has advised you on what you are signing up to.

A word (of warning) about joint venture partnerships

One of the things that we counsel our students against is entering joint venture (JV) partnerships with someone else on their projects (we're talking here about people other than a spouse or a close relative). That's not to say that all JVs turn bad or that they should be considered beyond the pale. But if we've told our students all the reasons why they shouldn't do them, then they're going to be proceeding with a lot more caution if they do eventually decide to partner up with someone.

A JV is when two or more people have a stake in the project's profits. Typical examples are when you team up with a friend or someone who brings experience and knowledge to the party. Similarly, it could also be with someone who has money or is the owner of the property or land to be developed. In most cases, it's likely to be an equal partnership where you each take 50% of the profits (or bear 50% of any losses). On paper, such an arrangement can look attractive and reassuring. After all, if there are two of you, then it certainly feels like it's not all down to you, plus it can be more fun to share the journey with someone else. And on the skills side, how great would it be to JV with an estate agent who might be able to get you great deals, a contractor who knows the industry inside out, or a financier who can put in all the money?

The problem that we see most frequently with JV partnerships is that the two parties involved don't have the same agenda or, in some cases, the same values. Often, they don't know each other well enough (if at all). We've seen partners clash because one of them perceived they were doing more than their fair share of the work. Others discovered that their partner was a complete control freak, a loose cannon, or a crook. Another common scenario is where one of the partners experiences an unexpected event in their lives and wants to pull out or at least pull back from the partnership. What happens then? The problem in these scenarios is that you only account for 50% of the decision-making authority. We recall one case where, unbeknown to one partner, the other (less experienced) partner had visited the site. The contractor had made some great recommendations about upgrading materials and adding new features, which all sounded absolutely spiffing, so the partner obligingly agreed to it. Months later, when the bill came in, the contractor's profits were up significantly (they could charge what they liked for the extras), and the developers' profits had dipped by a corresponding amount. An awkward moment, but at least the marble worktops looked lovely (and the contractor didn't go bust ☺).

Failed JV partnerships are one of the biggest issues we see in the world of small-scale developments, and the question we always ask people is why they feel it's necessary to joint venture. Do you really want to give away half of your profits when you can get the services or the finance you need by simply paying a fee to someone who has professional liability cover and isn't going to have a hissy fit over your kitchen worktop choice, defraud you, or make stupid decisions?

But hold on, surely working with a contractor would be a good thing as you'd get competitive pricing, plus you can guarantee you won't get ripped off? Wrong on both counts, unfortunately. Joint venturing with a contractor is probably the worst thing you can do, and here's why. A contractor in this scenario has two profit centres: their contracting business and their partnership with you. So, the first question; should you run a competitive tender to make sure that your partner's pricing is sharp, or do you go with whatever they want to charge? And, in any event, what happens if they start with competitive pricing but later make you aware of an 'unavoidable' cost increase that they must pass onto the project?

Suddenly your half of the profits are taking a hit, while your partner is alright, Jack, because they can effectively mitigate their position by charging what they like as the project's contractor. Surely you won't be standing for that! But hold on a minute, you only have half the vote, so the decision isn't yours alone, plus you can't out-vote them. Shall we see what your JV partner thinks about it? Hmm... Hopefully, you can see that JVing with a contractor places you at considerable risk. In most cases, you'd be far better simply hiring a contractor and a decent Project Manager to oversee them.

So, there you have it; our words of warning about joint ventures. But here's another way of looking at it, in case you're still sitting on the fence. In your current day job, would you be prepared to give us half your income or salary in return for doing half your work for you? We suspect not. After all, why would you only want to earn half as much money? And what if we did a rubbish job and put your career or business at risk? It doesn't sound that attractive, does it? Yet it's pretty much what a joint venture looks like.

But here's the thing; some joint ventures can work out fantastically well and deliver all of the benefits you'd hoped for. So, do your due diligence and make sure that you're 110% confident you're partnering with the right person before you jump in.

Build to rent

With a build to sell strategy, your units will typically be up for sale at the earliest opportunity. Once sold, you can then start paying back your commercial lender and your private investors, before pocketing the remainder as profit. Remember that all these transactions will be happening within your SPV limited company. Once all the units are sold, you will simply close the SPV and transfer the profits to yourself (or to your holding company).

With build to rent, you're going to be retaining the units and renting them out. Typically, you will be obtaining your development finance and buy-to-let mortgage from different lenders, which means you'll be using the latter to pay off the former. However, recently there has been an increase in the number of specialist build to let development lending products, where the finance for both the development and buy-to-let is provided within a single product.

In this chapter, we've focused on the finance side of development and hopefully given you some comfort that there is lots of money out there and that a developer with a great opportunity will be very much in demand. Of course, this then begs another question, namely, where can the aspiring small-scale developer lay their hands on some great deals? Which as luck would have it is exactly where we're heading off to next.

12. How Will I Find A Great Project?

Sources of deals

Finding deals is one of the critical aspects of being a property developer that you can't readily outsource. In your role as a property CEO, many things will happen automatically once a project starts moving forward. But in the early stages, it's largely going to be down to you to both find a good deal and evaluate it. In this chapter, we'll be running through the best places to find deals and looking at their respective pros and cons. It's highly advisable to pursue more than one strategy to maximise your chances of getting a deal.

A key point to remember is that searching for deals is like panning for gold. You're not trying to find fifty profitable deals. In fact, you're only trying to find one deal, but that deal could well end up netting you a six-figure profit. This is just as well, since finding great deals isn't easy. Ironically, this is good news because if it were, then every man, woman, and their dog would become a property developer. Instead, many people find it too hard to find a deal, so they give up, which means more opportunity for the educated and persistent developer, i.e., you.

Where should I be looking?

First things first, whichever source you tap into, you'll need to be clear on what it is you're looking for. There are three elements that you'll need to specify, which are location, property type, and budget. Let's start with location.

You will typically be looking in a fairly broad area, usually much wider than if you were looking for somewhere to live. Often this is driven by the practicalities of travel, for example you may want the project to be within an hour's drive of your home. You're going to have to be able to specify your search area, so you should translate 'an hour's drive from home' into a geographic area that you can relay to an agent or enter into a search portal.

Ultimately, it's up to you how far you want to travel, but bear in mind that, while you will need to visit the site occasionally, it's not a trip you'll be making every week. You'll want your search area to be wide enough to give you access to a reasonable number of potential deals, but not so broad that you struggle to find the time to search it properly. Remember that you'll be looking to maintain regular contact with the commercial agents in your search area, so don't bite of more than you can chew. By all means start with a smaller area and then work outwards.

There's an advantage in picking an area that you know well, and many of our students have search areas that lie further afield, often a place they have a historical connection to, for example where they grew up. Again, just be mindful of the travel times. Not only will you have to visit the site once you own it, but you may also need to do viewings at short notice when something comes onto the market.

Another good idea is to have a second, smaller search area, where your search can be either more detailed, or where you're looking for a more specific type of opportunity (or both). A good example of this would be looking for industrial conversion opportunities in your local town or city. It's an area you know very well, and it's small enough for you to search more intensively, including approaching owners directly and walking the streets. This is much more difficult to do in your wider search area due to its size.

What type of property should I be looking for?

There are some distinct advantages in having a niche. A key one is that you can become more of an expert in 'sweating the asset'. Each type of conversion has its nuances, and so a retail conversion opportunity differs to an office conversion and an industrial conversion, even if the basics are the same for each. There's no harm in being known as a specialist on one particular conversion type as it makes it easier for agents to remember you, plus you can get really good at doing them profitably.

Niching can also be driven by permitted development rights. For example, we have several students who specialise in converting agricultural buildings into residential using PDR class 'Q'. They've invested the time and effort to understand how the PDR works and where the best opportunities are. As a result, they're now very adept at understanding what a good opportunity looks like, which makes their search parameters quite specific. Perhaps the most common PDR-related niche is class MA, however it may still pay to niche down one step further into a particular type of building e.g. shops, banks, light industrial, etc. That said, there's no harm in looking for any type of commercial conversion, if you're wanting to see the maximum number of properties and keep your options open.

One newbie error to avoid is the good old FOMO search. This is where a new developer, fearing that they might miss out on a great opportunity if they narrow things down too much, tells an agent 'I'll look at anything that makes a 20% profit'. This is a quick route onto the agent's 'time-wasters' database and should be avoided at all costs. Do not let these words pass your lips.

On the other hand, don't be too specific. While you may be looking for something very particular, if you give too much detail to the agent, they'll simply send you either nothing or everything. They don't have the resources (or inclination) to filter out properties based on very exacting criteria, so just make sure your parameters are broad enough to be a reasonable filter that they can easily apply. You can always filter what they send you, but you can't if they don't send you anything.

When you use any of the online search portals, you'll need to specify your search parameters and apply any filters from a given range. You should assume that these are sensible parameters to give your agents too.

How big a budget should I set?

Your budget will be driven primarily by one of several things, which could include:

- the size of the project you're looking to tackle, i.e. the number of units you want to build
- the profit you want to make
- financial limitations, e.g. the amount of money you personally want to invest, the amount of private finance you wish to use, or any restrictions relating to commercial finance

There was once a rule of thumb that many people used when splitting the value of a conversion project into its component parts, namely:

- one third asset cost
- one third development cost
- one third profit

Some estate agents still like to quote this, which is a tad unfair on developers. In these enlightened times, looking for a 33% profit, while not impossible by any means, certainly sits at the optimistic end of the scale. You'll be looking for a 20% profit as a minimum, so we would expect the more accurate ratios to be:

- 33-40% asset cost
- 33-40% development cost
- 20-30% profit

Clearly the actual ratios on any given project could be significantly different, mainly dependent on the scale of the construction work involved. However, this broad-brush approach at least allows us to work out a ball-park budget for the asset we're going to buy. We can do this based on the profit we're looking to make e.g. if we want to make £200k profit, then our asset will cost around £350-400k. We can use the same ratio to work back from a GDV. So, for example, if you wanted to build a maximum of ten units, and you knew the average sales price of a flat you would build would be £100k, then your GDV would be £1m and your asset price can be calculated based on the same ratios mentioned previously.

It's not designed to be an exact science, but since you will need to have a specific search budget, it pays dividends to have a reasonable idea before you start looking. You can always refine your criteria as you go forward, but it's probably best to start with too wide a search and then narrow it down, rather than the other way around.

For new build opportunities, the ratios will be different since the land cost is likely to make up a smaller proportion of the overall cost and the construction cost will be greater. Another complication will be buying land where planning permission has already been granted, since this can have a markedly higher value.

There are some additional considerations that you may want to take into account:

- We recommend making your first project as easy as possible, so it can be completed quickly and with minimum risk. As a result, you may want to set your search parameters lower on your first outing
- Your broker will give you a steer on what loan values lenders will be prepared to offer you, and this too may have an influence on your budget. You'll find that lenders often set a minimum loan value, since larger loans take no more work on their part, but produce more profit

So, now we have our three basic search parameters, we can start looking. Let's run through the best places to search.

Online portals

Arguably the best part of being a modern small-scale property developer is the sheer amount of work you can get done in your pyjamas. There was a time back in the dark ages (ok, the nineties) when stuff only tended to get done during working hours, which for most people was 9 to 5. This made property development difficult for those with careers because by the time they'd clocked out of the day job of an evening, so had most estate agents.

Roll the clock forward to today, and you can surf the internet to your heart's content, marvelling at the bevy of properties available not only on the estate agents' website but also on property portals like Rightmove, Estates Gazette, and Zoopla. This is a game-changer because it means we can search for properties (and do our desktop due diligence and research) at a time to suit us, day or night.

We would recommend using the following online resources:

- Your local agents' websites (don't assume that their deals will always appear on the portals in a timely fashion),
- Rightmove (www.rightmove.co.uk) – select 'Commercial' from the main menu
- Zoopla (www.zoopla.co.uk) – select 'Commercial' from the main menu
- Estates Gazette (www.estatesgazette.co.uk)

How do you get the best out of these websites? Luckily there's no rocket science involved:

- Register as a user on each portal – it's free
- Save your searches – this will save time as it will mean you won't have to re-enter your search parameters every time you access the site
- Where possible, sign up for email alerts – this will ensure you get notified of potential deals as soon as they are put on the portal

We'd still recommend a weekly visit to each portal, even where you have alerts set up. Not only does this allow you to see what's been sold since you last looked, but we're also not convinced that their email alerts are 100% fool proof, so a regular check will ensure you don't miss anything.

Now, we'd love to tell you that all you need to do is scan these websites, and all the deals you could want will miraculously appear. But that would be way too easy; in fact, most seasoned developers don't go anywhere near these websites.

So why are we telling you to use them? All will hopefully become clear over the following pages.

Commercial estate agents

If we had to pick only one route for sourcing deals, using commercial agents would win hands down. But hang on a second; we've just told you to scan the estate agents' website, so surely that means you don't need to do anything else? Won't you get to find out about all their properties by looking at their websites? The answer is 'not by a long way'. Let us explain why.

The process that most people would assume happens every time a property comes on to the market with either a commercial or residential estate agent is as follows. Things start with the agent getting a call from the vendor. So, let's assume that Donna, the vendor, has just contacted Michael, the agent because she wants to sell her old printing works. Michael pops over to view the property and makes all the right noises about selling it quickly and getting a reasonable price. Donna likes the cut of Michael's jib, so they shake hands, and Michael gets appointed as the sole selling agent. All very straightforward so far.

Michael then heads back to the office where he has a chat with Arthur and Martha, his office juniors, and briefs them about Donna and her printing works. Arthur and Martha are duly dispatched to the property to measure up and take photos. They then return to the office and set about creating an entry for the property on their agency's website plus they create listings on Rightmove, Zoopla, and Estates Gazette. They also arrange for an email to be sent to their database, notifying potential buyers that Donna's printing works is on the market.

The next step sees potential buyers get in contact with the agency. Michael talks to each one, briefing them on the property and establishing each buyer's position. Where a viewing is arranged, Michael will drive out to Donna's printing works and show each potential buyer around. And if he's lucky, he won't have to have too many phone conversations or do too many viewings before someone makes an acceptable offer.

That's the process that most people would guess happens in every estate agency up and down the land, and they'd not be too far wrong. Let's call this default sales process 'Route One'. But Route One isn't the estate agents' preferred approach, not by a long way. Let's look at what really happens.

The first part is exactly the same; Michael has a call from Donna and having viewed the property, it's agreed that Michael will sell her printing works for her. But instead of heading back to the office to brief Arthur and Martha, Michael parks himself around the corner, digs out his address book (yes, the estate agent's famous 'black book'), and makes a series of phone calls.

His first call is to Tim, a buyer who Michael knows is looking for a commercial property in the area, and for whom Donna's printing works is not only ideal, it's also well within Tim's budget.

"Hi Tim, it's Michael here. How are things with you? I thought I'd give you a quick call because I've just taken on a property that I think you might be interested in taking a look at..."

Michael proceeds to give Tim the lowdown on the printing works and answers Tim's questions.

"At this stage, the property isn't on the open market. I'm just calling a handful of buyers who I know will be interested, and you were top of my list. If you're interested, I can meet you at the property first thing tomorrow morning and show you around. How does that sound?"

A viewing is arranged, and Michael says goodbye to Tim and hangs up. He then locates another name in his black book and makes a second, almost identical call to another 'hot' buyer.

Let's pause things there to understand what's going on. Michael already knows of Tim, and equally importantly, he knows that Donna's printing works is a property that Tim would be interested in buying. In fact, Michael knows half a dozen 'hot buyers' like Tim who are likely to be interested in buying a property like Donna's. And of the six people he rings, four can do a viewing the very next day. A day after that, Michael's had offers in from three of them and, having discussed these with Donna, she accepts one of them (in case you're already fully engaged with the characters and interested in knowing how this entirely fictional story pans out, we can tell you that, yes, Tim was the successful bidder ☺).

As you can see, it's quite a different process to Route One that we discussed earlier, and from Michael's perspective, a much more efficient one. Arthur and Martha were not called into action. There was no measuring up, nor were any photos taken. The particulars were not put in the estate agent's window. No details of the property were circulated online, so Messrs Rightmove, Zoopla, and Estates Gazette didn't get a whiff of the deal. And Michael didn't have to take lots of phone calls or do lots of viewings. He's not only quids in, but he's also saved himself a lot of hard work. And, because it only took him 48 hours to sell Donna's property, he'll be getting his commission payment that much sooner.

Donna is also happy; she managed to sell her property within just two days of appointing Michael, and she was able to receive three good offers from serious buyers. And of course, Tim is over the moon; he's just secured his first development deal. All of the effort spent building a relationship with Michael has just paid off.

A few things should also be apparent. Firstly, this 'black book' sales process will be every estate agent's preferred way of selling property. After all, it's far more economical and quicker than Route One, and so almost every estate agent will initially look to go down this avenue to start with. Why do Rightmove, Zoopla, and Estates

Gazette have any listings if every agent finds buyers through their black book? The answer, of course, is that this black book process doesn't guarantee a successful sale. What if Tim and his fellow hot buyers weren't that interested in Donna's printing works? Maybe the asking price was too steep, or the property wasn't quite right for them. Or maybe Donna felt she could get a better price by putting her property in front of a bigger audience. Guess what Michael does then? Absolutely right, he reverts to Route One. Arthur and Martha rock up with tape measure and camera in hand, and the property goes on the open market.

There's another thing that should be apparent, and it involves a couple of characters we've not yet mentioned, Maisie and Dave. So how do they fit in? Well, Maisie met with Michael some six months previously. Having told him what she was looking for, she now receives regular emails from Arthur and Martha every time Michael's agency takes on a property that meets her criteria. Donna's printing works would have been a perfect fit for Maisie. But Michael meets a lot of potential buyers and someone who spoke to him six months ago but hasn't been in touch since just isn't going to make it into his little black book. I mean, they can't be that serious, can they? The truth is he can barely remember Maisie, even though she's on his mailing list.

And as for Dave, what was he up to? Well, Dave's not daft. What's the point wasting time speaking to agents when they put all their properties on the internet for everyone to see anyway? So, when Michael was calling Tim to tell him all about the printing works opportunity, Dave was in his pyjamas eating a bowl of cornflakes, glued to Rightmove, Zoopla, and Estates Gazette, ready to pounce just as soon as the right property appeared. Oops.

Our estate agency friends conservatively reckon that over half of all properties are sold using their little black books or an equivalent 'off-market' process. And of course, it's arguably the better half since properties only appear on the internet if they fail to be sold any other way. You won't be surprised to learn that one of the first things we teach new students is not only how to build relationships with agents but specifically how to get into their little black book of hot buyers. Won't this be difficult to do for a newbie developer? Not if you know how to build a brand, understand how to build rapport with agents, and look like the consummate professional you are.

One final tip with regards to commercial agents is to use a CRM (Customer Relationship Management) tool to manage your follow-up dialogue. It can be all too easy to lose track of what properties they've sent you and when you should next call them, particularly when you've dozens of agent relationships on the go. CRM apps are usually inexpensive (some are free) and you can use them to set yourself email reminders etc. to systemise your follow-up campaigns. You can also use the same CRM tool to manage your deals.

Residential agents

Residential estate agents play a crucial role in the life of most developers as they will typically sell your end product. While some developers specialise in refurbishing or extending existing residential property, most will opt for either residential new build or some type of commercial, industrial, or agricultural conversion to residential. These will typically be sold to us by commercial agents, so why do residential agents feature on our deal sourcing list?

The answer lies in networking. Experienced residential agents are part of the local property community and often hear about non-residential land or premises that may be coming onto the market. And if you're going to be developing residential units, you will also need to forge relationships with the people who will sell them. This is an excellent opportunity to explain what type of deal you are looking for and ask them to contact you if they hear of anything of interest. It's also worth mentioning that many estate agent firms have both a commercial and residential sales arm.

Auctioneers

Auction houses should be on your shopping list, although you should proceed with caution as they are a unique buying experience. Here are our golden rules:

- If you're thinking of bidding at an auction, make sure you do a dry run first. Go to an auction and get a feel for the place. See how the auctioneer works the room and how people bid. It's a very different environment, and you'll want to experience it before you start bidding for real
- Get to know the auctioneer. They're always keen to meet new customers, and they can sometimes give you a steer on what's happening with individual lots
- Set a limit and stick to it. The auctioneer's job is to persuade you to part with more cash, and it's all too easily done. You've probably heard the expression 'you make your money when you buy, not when you sell', and it's very true. Given that you'll have done a fair amount of analysis and due diligence to reach the point where you're bidding on a property, you might be tempted to bid that little bit more just to secure it. Don't; instead, stipulate a ceiling price you won't go above and walk away if you reach it
- Get familiar with the legals. The buying process at an auction is different from buying through an estate agent, so make sure you're up to speed. Most auctioneers will have a comprehensive guide available on their website
- See if you can do a pre-auction deal. There's nothing quite so frustrating as attending an auction, having done all your due diligence, only to find that the lot you were interested

in has been withdrawn. Why has this happened? Chances are, some enterprising developer has got in early and done a deal with the vendor by contacting the auctioneer. There's no reason this can't be you, although there's no guarantee that the vendor won't still want to take their chances on getting a better price at auction.

Be aware that when the hammer falls you are obligated to buy and will need to put down an immediate deposit and be able to complete quickly, often within 28 days.

Direct to vendor

In many respects, direct to vendor (DTV) can justifiably be considered the 'hard yards' of finding property development deals. What exactly is DTV? It's where you, the developer, approach a property owner (or landowner) whose property isn't currently for sale and ask them to sell it to you.

Well, no wonder it's hard then, we hear you say. Why on earth would you waste your time trying to buy property from people who don't want to sell? Ok, let's imagine for a moment that you currently own your home, and you're NOT looking to sell it. In fact, you're very happy chez nous; the kids are settled, you've made wonderful friends here, the local pub does a Sunday roast to die for, etc. A blissful existence. And then one day, you're approached by a local property developer who says that they're very keen to acquire your lovely home because they want to knock it down and build something else.

Now, obviously, your answer will be 'no thank you, we don't want to move.' Until that is, the developer discloses that they would be willing to pay you 50% more than your house is currently worth for the privilege. Now, all of a sudden, they have your attention. In an instant, the kids are very resilient to change, your friends will always be friends, and surely there will be other pubs that do a nice roast.

I mean, think what you could do with the extra cash. Or think of the even better house or neighbourhood you could now afford to move to. The thing is, it's a time-limited offer. The developer isn't going to wait around forever for you to decide. So, you have to choose now whether to grab the opportunity or stay put.

Why is the developer able to offer you so much? It's because they know how to maximise the value of the house or its land and will be able to make even more profit by developing it. Their numbers stack up even after paying you over the odds for your home. And hopefully, you can see how it could be a powerful motivation for people to accept such an offer, despite not currently having their home on the market. Most properties are theoretically for sale; it's simply a question of what price their owners are willing to accept for them.

The same process is in play when you approach landowners or commercial building owners directly. In essence, you'll be able to offer them more than they believe their property is worth on the open market, which will encourage them to consider selling it to you. This all sounds great in principle, but how can you afford to pay a premium for their property? The answer is that you'll have an edge. You'll know how to maximise the value of a property so that it will be worth significantly more after you've finished developing it. And this will allow you to pay more than the property is worth in its current state and still make a healthy profit.

Ok, but precisely what edge did we have in mind? Let's consider a fairly typical example. Derek owns a small light industrial building (but it could equally be an office, a shop, or other non-residential premises). It sits in a residential street, and, as Derek would be the first to admit, it could probably do with a lick of paint and a bit of tidying up here and there. It's not derelict by any stretch, but anyone that bought it would need to spend a few bob knocking it back into shape. Why hasn't Derek done it? Well, he doesn't need to. He'll be retiring in a few years and doesn't have the desire or the cash to renovate the place. He's not thinking of selling just yet because he's still using it. He suspects he'll sell up when he retires, and the building will be worth what any business will be willing to pay, given that it needs a bit of work doing to it.

Enter the heroine of our story, Jenny. Jenny's a small-scale property developer. She specialises in using permitted development rights (PDRs) to convert commercial buildings into residential (she could convert it into any number of other uses, but let's stick to residential for this example). She's very interested in Derek's building because she knows she can convert it using Permitted Development Rights. Six flats, to be precise, and each one slap bang in the middle of an up-and-coming residential area. She's done her homework and knows what the apartments will sell for, what they will cost to build, and therefore how much she can afford to pay Derek. She's also done her homework on Derek's property, so she knows how much it's worth on the open market as a commercial building. So, even before she's contacted Derek, she already knows that she can afford to pay him significantly more than the building is worth.

You can probably imagine the thoughts that went through Derek's mind after Jenny had made contact. He was intrigued. After all, it was a no-lose situation; if he didn't sell to Jenny, then he wouldn't lose anything. But was Jenny legitimate? A quick look on her website suggested she was. He even recognised the local architect, which her website stated was one of her team, and a quick call confirmed that Jenny was the genuine article. So, what should he do? Here was a one-off opportunity to make a not-insignificant amount of money by selling out to a developer. What could this mean? Early retirement? Relocation? A nest egg in the bank?

Now we won't play out the Jenny and Derek story any further because, of course, there could be thousands of different potential scenarios when it comes to a building's owner's situation. Plus, you may only have just recovered from the cut and thrust of our earlier Tim and Michael saga ☺. Different people or businesses own different buildings, all with different personal or commercial situations. But hopefully, you understand why DTV deals can work; the developer can afford to pay more because they have an edge, and the building's owner is faced with a no-lose situation that could create a significant windfall.

An important final point; in theory, Derek could potentially do some research, discover permitted development rights, and learn how to become a property developer himself. He would then be in the same position as Jenny. So, why doesn't this happen? Firstly, Derek doesn't know what he doesn't know. He wouldn't know how to find out why Jenny could afford to pay more for his property. In the same way that, if a developer was to knock on your own front door, you probably wouldn't think 'I wonder how I could develop my house, instead of accepting the developer's offer'. Indeed, Derek may think she's simply paying over the odds by mistake. Secondly, he has no intention of learning how to develop property. He already has a business to run and doesn't want to start another one. Similarly, Derek may have already thought about developing his property and either talked to some agents or approached some developers. But, because they all assumed that the existing structure would need to be knocked down and then rebuilt, the numbers didn't stack up. Again, they didn't know what they didn't know, namely that it was possible to convert the existing building using PDRs. So, Jenny not only had an edge on Derek, but she also had an edge on her competitors.

Professionals

As a developer, you'll have a team of professionals that work for you. And, as we mentioned earlier, these people are not your employees; they're people or businesses that you contract with to build a specific project. Of course, each professional team member also works with many other developers, and they're well integrated into the local property development landscape. So, do you think they might hear about development opportunities that come up locally? Of course, they will. And why might they relay these opportunities to you? Well, guess who's likely to get the gig if you win the deal? <u>They</u> will. And who's going to earn a lot of brownie points with you, their customer, if they find you a deal? Yep, it's the same answer. So, it's well worth asking your professional team to keep an ear to the ground for opportunities that meet your discerning criteria, so they can let you know if any cross their path.

Your network

The power of a good network is that it can extend way beyond its immediate circle. If you know fifty people and each of those people knows fifty others, you'll have access to 2,500 people in addition to the fifty you already know, providing you can tap into that broader network.

That's all very well, but what use are 2,500 people to you as a property developer? Interestingly, most new developers start by thinking that they don't know many people who could be helpful to them. What constitutes being helpful to a property developer? Several things spring to mind:

They may have a property to sell or that you could potentially offer on. Like money, people tend not to talk much about the property they own, which is why it's critical you position yourself correctly. As developers, it can be tempting to think of our customers as the people who will ultimately buy the homes that we build. In reality, we need to be looking up the chain rather than down it to identify who our customers are. Our customers should include:

- Private investors looking for a good return
- Professionals looking for a new project

- Property owners looking to sell their property

The critical issue is to make sure that you position yourself as a property solutions provider and not just a developer. Not only do you need to tell everyone about what your development business does, but you need to make it relevant to them. How does your business solve their problem? A would-be investor may not be interested in buying the flats you've just built, but they might well be interested in securing an 8-10% return on their investment. Likewise, if your network knows someone with a property they may be interested in selling, you want to be very clear that that's precisely what you do. So, you're providing solutions up the chain, as well as down it.

They could be potential private investors. As we mentioned previously, people you either know directly or who are connected to you by an acquaintance can be excellent sources of private finance, even if you never knew they had money to invest.

They may know professionals and potential NEAs. You'll ideally be building your professional team based on personal recommendations, and there will be people in your network who can connect you to people they'd recommend.

They say one's network is one's net worth, and it's essential that developers recognise the value of growing their network. It shouldn't be a passive thing, where you simply leverage the contacts you already have. You want to be out there creating new connections.

How do you do this? There are a couple of key strategies that will serve you well. The first is to tell everybody what you do (and do this at every available opportunity). The second is to make networking part of your calendar; in other words, force yourself to go to events where you can network.

What are the best events for property developers to go to? The pick of the bunch has to be business networking events. These can take various forms, from nationwide business networking organisations to local business meets and Chambers of Commerce. The advantage of business networking groups is that you may well be the only developer in the room, plus many of the people you will talk to will be business owners. What do business owners have that could interest a developer? Well, they'll own commercial property for one. But they're also likely to have funds to invest. And if you're the only property developer in the room, you have something of a monopoly.

Property networking events can also be helpful, although many are run by property training organisations, and you may find the crowd is more interested in rental strategies (e.g., buy-to-lets, HMOs, serviced accommodation, etc.) rather than development.

Many local areas have unique property networking events for those involved in the business. These can range from formal events hosted by local organisations to a monthly pub meet-up. You should interrogate your professional team to find out where the local developers, estate agents, architects, and other professionals hang out.

One of the best networking strategies you can deploy is to offer to speak at a networking event (we can see you visibly recoil at the thought of public speaking, but please hear us out). Speaking at an event places you in a position of authority. Everyone will assume you must be an expert because what sort of fool volunteers to speak in front of an audience if they don't know what they're talking about (we'll exclude politicians from this analogy, just to be on the safe side)? The good news is that you don't need to talk about development, which may be just as well if you're just starting. You can talk about any subject that you think will interest your audience; it could be business-related or about having the right mindset to overcome challenges. Or it could be about you and your business journey and what you've learned on the way. The point is you'll be able to position yourself as a property developer, and your audience will view you as a subject matter expert.

Property sourcers

These people find deals, 'package' them, and then sell them on to developers for a fee. A good sourcer will not only have found an off-market property, but they will also have negotiated a price with the vendor and done all of the necessary groundwork to secure the property and facilitate the sale. They then receive a fee from the developer once the sale is complete.

Property sourcers can be a mixed bag, with some doing a better job of 'packaging' than others. That said, it costs nothing to have sourcers send you opportunities, so there is no harm in having a few in your contacts list. You will, of course, have to factor their fee into your deal analysis, but that's not a problem if the deal still stacks. Plus, they can save you a significant amount of time and effort if they find you a great deal. Just make sure that they're not your only source of potential deals.

Creating a system

We've now covered the main places you should be looking for deals. We mentioned that building good relationships with commercial agents was our preferred approach, but we also suggested that you should employ multiple strategies. Hopefully, you now also appreciate that looking for deals on the property portals can still pay huge dividends because, with a little knowledge, it's entirely possible for you to see an angle that your competitors haven't seen. Agents will have a relatively small number of hot buyers, and there's certainly a fair chance that none of them have seen how to make the opportunity stack up. So don't give up on your pyjama-clad searches just yet.

One of the problems that arises when looking for opportunities is something we call 'deal blindness'. Look at five deals in detail, and you'll most likely be able to remember the salient points of each. But once you're up to ten deals, things will start to become a little blurred. And after twenty or thirty deals, you'll have no chance of remembering all the details of every opportunity you've analysed.

Why is this important? It's because situations change. A property that went under offer six weeks ago may suddenly come back on the market when the deal falls through, and the agent calls you. In this situation, you'll want to move quickly. You don't want to have to be scratching your head, desperately trying to remember the analysis you did or the decision you reached six weeks ago. The answer, then, is to make sure that you have a GREAT filing system for all your deals. You need to be able to quickly pick up the threads without having to redo all your groundwork from scratch.

It also means making sure that you've documented where you've got to on each deal once you've finished analysing it. Our minds play tricks on us; when we've just finished looking at a deal, we'll be super-confident that we'll remember every detail. Roll the clock forward six months, and you'll struggle to recall what the building looks like, let alone why you didn't proceed with it. So, make sure that your filing system includes a place to record your findings and your assessment of every deal you look at. This doesn't have to be the complete works of Shakespeare – a simple paragraph or two should do the job.

We also strongly recommend that you create a deal assessment checklist that you use on every deal you look at. This is simply a list of factors you need to consider as part of your deal assessment process. You don't want to be relying on your memory each time you look at a deal, and the checklist ensures that you never miss anything out.

Premium property data applications and software

There are various software applications you can purchase that allow you to take shortcuts to obtain property information on any given geographical area. The applications can vary, with some providing information on ownership, planning history and the like, while other focus more on providing market sales data and trends. The main advantage they all give you is in saving you time, since the information itself is usually in the public domain, just not in one place. In other words, you can access all the information they give you elsewhere for free, but it will take you longer. Personally, we like the time-saving aspect so we're big fans, but for those on a budget, these apps are not essential.

Most of these applications charge a monthly or annual subscription fee, in some cases, quite a significant one. We're not going to explore the pros and cons of each one here, and if you can afford them, they will certainly make things easier/quicker for you, plus they can give you some additional information that could be useful to you.

However, we would offer some words of caution if you were thinking about exclusively using them for data analysis:

1. Most of these apps don't provide a qualitative assessment of properties. For example, when telling you the average selling price of flats locally, an old two-bedroom ex-council flat that sold for £100k might be in the same data pool as a brand new two-bedroom penthouse flat with parking and gym access that sold for £500k. Not only is their average sales price of £300k essentially meaningless, you probably wouldn't want to include either property in your analysis, as they are both outliers

2. Similarly, because you're not seeing any images of properties currently for sale when you look at app data, you're not getting a picture of the quality of finish, style, or kerb appeal of the competition
3. Many apps don't offer the degree of granularity you need, e.g. they give you average values for 2-bed properties, but don't distinguish between flats and houses, let alone penthouses and bedsits
4. Finally, we'd suggest you still need to know how you can get the data manually, even if you also use other tools

Consider outsourcing

The harsh reality of finding deals is that you're most likely going to have to kiss a lot of frogs before you find your princess or prince. Of course, you could get lucky and find a great deal immediately, but the odds are somewhat stacked against it. You won't be thinking this at the time, but it's actually a good thing, as we mentioned before. It means that of all those would-be developers, your competition, who thought they'd 'give development a go', many will simply give up and go home instead. But because you have a great system, plus you have an edge and know how to analyse deals, you'll stick with it, and you'll ultimately find one. And once you've completed one development project, finding a second becomes a lot easier because more deals will come to you rather than you having to go looking for them.

Given that deal sourcing is down to you as the CEO, how can you make life easier for yourself? One way is to hire a virtual assistant to help you. Strictly speaking, they don't need to be virtual, but as the gig economy has expanded, it's given developers an excellent opportunity to recruit people on an ad hoc basis without having to employ them directly. It can also be very cost-effective.

It's a simple enough proposition. People who are available to work will register their CVs on search portals, as do 'employers' (i.e., you) who are looking to outsource some work, whether it's a one-off job or an ongoing role. Examples include portals such as peopleperhour.com, fiverr.com, and upwork.com. If someone likes the sound of your job, they'll reply to your post, and you can effectively interview them. The essential advantage of this model is that these workers can be based anywhere in the world. Not only does this give you a lot of potential candidates, but their hourly rates are also likely to be much lower if they're based in countries with lower living costs. The trade-off is that their language skills might not be native quality, and they'll be operating in different time zones. However, you're not confined to recruiting overseas people; you can select home-based talent, albeit it may cost more.

While you don't want your virtual assistants to be making qualitative decisions on deals, there's quite a lot of more routine work they could tackle for you on the deal sourcing side. This includes:

- identifying agents and contacts
- contacting agents and arranging meetings or viewings on your behalf
- managing your CRM system for both contacts and deals

It would be possible for the more skilled virtual assistant to obtain information from the internet to populate your deal analysers, albeit some training on your part would be required. They could also research off-market DTV deals for you.

The trick is to consider outsourcing everything. We tend to do stuff ourselves because we perceive there's no one else who can do it. The reality is that there are many routine tasks that you could outsource. And if you bring on board some additional resources cost-effectively, it frees up your time to focus on the more important stuff, and your development journey proceeds more quickly as a result. And don't just think about outsourcing your property development tasks. If you can outsource domestic chores or other work tasks, you can spend the time you free up looking for your next deal.

So, you now know the best places to search for deals. But how will you know a good deal when you see one? And is there a way of making sure that you don't pick a deal that's going to lose you money?

Let's find out...

13. How Can I Be Confident I Won't Lose Money?

The due diligence process

Once we've found a deal, we need to do our due diligence to see if it stacks up. 'Stacking up' means that the deal will return a minimum 20% profit based on its GDV.

Unfortunately, it's not always possible to determine whether a deal stacks up just by looking at it on Rightmove; you may need to do a little investigating and number crunching first. And here's the surprising secret to running the numbers successfully; do NOT do it thoroughly.

While this sounds like a recipe for disaster, the problem with doing an in-depth analysis of every deal you look at is that it will take you forever. You'll spend ages crunching numbers on a deal only to find out that it doesn't stack, and the whole process will be horribly inefficient. It's far better to do your deal analysis in several stages, where you only pass to the next stage if the results from the previous stage look positive. Think of it like a funnel that your deals are passing through, with each stage more thorough than the last, but deals only progressing if they meet your required criteria. Here are the four number-crunching stages we would recommend:

1. EYEBALL: A high-level assessment without crunching any numbers

2. FIRST-PASS: A run through your generic deal analyser (you'll be using generic, high-level costing assumptions)

3. ESTIMATE: A more tailored analysis (you've changed some of the assumptions to reflect the specifics of the project, but they're still estimates). This is the minimum you would do before making an offer

4. CUSTOMISED: A fully customised analysis (you've got quotes for all the main pricing variables and are no longer using assumptions).

The sales funnel process involves analysing every deal one stage at a time and then ejecting it from the funnel if it doesn't look like it will stack up. By analysing in stages, we don't then spend time doing a complete, 'full-fat' analysis on every deal. Instead, we gradually eject deals from the process until we're only left with the most promising ones. That way, we're making the best use of our time and resources.

Your challenge is to spend as little time as possible on deals that don't stack up. You certainly never want to go to view a property unless you're confident that it has some potential, and the only way you'll know that is to crunch some numbers beforehand. Don't make the mistake of thinking that viewings are a great way of meeting agents. If you go on dozens of viewings and make zero offers, agents will quickly get the measure of you. Far better to go for quality rather than quantity and only view properties where making an offer is a realistic outcome. We would usually want to reach Stage 3 of our analysis before we went on a viewing. However, because this stage still uses estimates, you can reach it very quickly under your own steam, without waiting for other people to get back to you with prices or quotes.

It's worth noting that if you're not comfortable that your Stage 4 pricing is definitive enough, you may want to have further input from your team of professionals, e.g. structural engineers, M&E consultants, etc. in order to firm up the pricing, however, be aware that this may come at an additional cost.

What exactly is deal analysis?

While we're not going to dive into the detail of how to analyse deals in this book (that would need a separate book in its own right), we do want to cover the main principles and also share with you our set of golden rules that apply to deal analysis.

Deal analysis is part of your due diligence; the investigation and calculations that you do to determine whether a deal stacks up and whether or not you should bid for it, and if so, at what price. It's not a single piece of paper, nor is it a single calculation. It usually takes the form of several Excel worksheets that roll up into an executive summary, and it covers EVERY relevant aspect of a deal that you need to decide whether it stacks up.

Let's start by running through the golden rules of deal analysis.

The golden rules

Deal analysis MUST follow a system

Imagine cooking a recipe with a hundred ingredients that you were serving to someone important. What are the chances that you'd try and remember them all, together with their quantities and method, instead of referring to the recipe? Zero. Why? Because you know you wouldn't get it right – you'd always miss at least one or two out.

There are many parts to a development project, and if you forget to include one, it can be costly. What you don't want to do is rely on your memory. Instead, you need a systemised deal analysis process covering every relevant element. And that involves having a generic deal analysis spreadsheet.

Time is of the essence

Deals don't hang around; you need to move with speed but never at the expense of accuracy. By having a system, you're quickly able to work out whether a deal stacks up while being confident that you've considered every relevant factor. You want to have a deal analysed in a few hours and not a few days, to a point where you could make an offer. You only need to reach Stage 3 to make an offer; but you always need to reach Stage 4 before you purchase.

Computer says... build your own model

We suggest that while you could use someone else's model as a starting point, you should build your own deal analyser. Why? Well, other people's spreadsheets and tools are not guaranteed to be error-free. Plus, you may find yourself knowing that you need to put a specific figure in a particular cell, but you don't know why or what happens as a result. You need to understand how your spreadsheet works and be confident that any errors can only be yours and not someone else's. The exception would be where you've been given a deal analyser by a recognised training resource and have been taught how to use it. Even then, you should audit it and make sure you understand precisely how it works.

Keep it clean

Some people tend to be rather messy when it comes to spreadsheets and reports. They may have all the right numbers in the right places. And while THEY may know how to decipher the output, woe betide anyone else who tries to make sense of it.

Take the time to structure your analysers in a user-friendly way. Include a page of notes that explains what each calculation does. Imagine that you were going to give it to an (imaginary) colleague later on. It would have to be easy to use, obvious where everything goes and what data needs collecting. Plus, it would look comprehensive but clear (and easy on the eye) to whoever is reading it when you print it out. That's how you should build yours.

Why bother? Three key reasons:

- Your memory is not infallible, and if you have to revisit the analyser months from now, will you remember what went where?
- Someone on your team may need to understand how to use the spreadsheet to create, amend or understand what you've done
- The selected outputs from your deal analyser are a fantastic way to present deals to brokers and commercial/private investors. And this is the last place you want to look like you have a shambolic approach to your number crunching

Evolution is critical

So, is your deal analyser a set and forget? No chance. Your deal analyser is a living, breathing beast that grows with every deal you analyse. Never get the deal to fit the analyser; always get the analyser to fit the deal.

Again, make sure that you pay attention to the content and output when you expand your analyser. How easy will it be for someone to revisit the spreadsheet in the future to see what you did? Also, make sure that you maintain good version control by putting version numbers and dates on each evolution as you update it.

Detail is essential

The detail is where the devil lives, so you need to be able to see him. Never try and build a one-page summary of a deal directly. The final figures should result from the more detailed calculations that occur under the bonnet in other parts of the spreadsheet. In other words, let the detail drive the summary; don't try and build a summary from scratch.

You can't outsource deal analysis

Deal analysis is not something you can or should ever outsource to anyone else. Rubbish with spreadsheets? Tough luck – get good at them (you don't need to be a technical whiz). Find numbers confusing? Hard cheese – get to grips with them (the maths is not complicated). Tough love? You bet. Because only YOU can be responsible for doing a deal. You shouldn't delegate that role to anyone else, no matter how great they may be at numbers or spreadsheets. By all means, have someone check things over for you, but they're YOUR numbers, and the buck stops with you. You will have ZERO comeback if someone else runs your numbers incorrectly.

Best guesses are still guessing

A common error we see in deal analysis is where people don't check their numbers. You need facts or as close to them as you can get. Don't get lazy and stick with ball-park figures or assumptions in your Stage 4 numbers; take the trouble to firm them up. The fewer question marks you have, the less risk you'll have, and the more profitable you'll be.

We had a situation recently where a student had decided that the build cost per square metre given to them by their contractor on their most recent project would be a reasonable assumption to use. As it turned out, it wasn't. Not only was their contractor not available, but the market had also moved in the previous 6 months resulting in a material increase in labour costs. A quick phone call was all it took to find this out. Luckily, they didn't get as far as committing to the purchase before making that call.

Reasonableness testing and double-checking

It always pays to double-check your result by working the deal through manually. Once your deal analyser has given you a result, take a separate piece of paper and work out the numbers manually (rounding as necessary) to make sure the result you're getting from the deal analyser looks reasonable. If you get a materially different number, you'll want to go through your numbers again to find out why.

Why should you do this? One of the challenges with a complex model is that we tend to rely on the output. Yet we may have made a silly data entry error somewhere or overwritten a formula. Doing the exercise longhand, even if you ball-park some of the detail numbers, will allow you to check this. You're not trying to square things to the penny, but it should allow you to spot where there are any obvious discrepancies.

Also, make sure that you have audit checks embedded in your spreadsheet. These will flag where numbers either don't cross-cast or where they're unreasonable.

Finally, it's always helpful to have someone knowledgeable on your team check over the numbers before you make an offer. This will help ensure that you haven't missed or miscalculated anything.

Exercise good version control

You will doubtless end up with several versions of a deal analysis as you go through the various stages. This will either be because new data requires a new iteration or because you want to compare different what-if scenarios. Make sure that you not only number each version but also describe what each represents. There's nothing more frustrating than running many iterations and losing track of which one is which.

Cashflow is key

Ensure that you have modelled your project's cash flow on a separate tab to ensure you don't have any shortfall during the project. Many a deal has foundered where the number in the

229

bottom right-hand corner looked great, but there wasn't enough cash available to get there.

Always perform what-if scenarios

Not all your numbers will be cast in stone. What happens if your contractor goes bust and their replacement charges 10% more? What if your GDVs are affected by a market change that sees them drop by 10%?

You need to run what-if scenarios/sensitivity analyses to see how your numbers look if you encounter a bump in the road. A deal that only stacks up when things turn out perfectly is not a real deal. Rest assured, your commercial lenders will be using similar what-if tests to try and break your deal. You want to do the same.

Avoid optimism

So, you've finished entering your numbers into the deal analyser, and the computer says 'no'. But hold on a second; it's only a few percentage points off being doable. Maybe you were a bit overcautious? What if you didn't need quite such a large contingency? Or perhaps you could manage to shave another £5 per square foot off the build cost? And who needs tarmac when you can have gravel?

Welcome to the slippery slope that is optimistic assumptions. We can get every deal we look at to stack up if we're optimistic on all the assumptions, which should tell you something. Where you have facts, don't try and be optimistic; you'll be basing it on chance. Where you've had to make assumptions because you don't have facts, and you've been prudent, then be sensible. For sure, if every assumption is dialled to maximum prudence, then you'll find that none of your deals stack up. The reality is that some costs will come in higher and others lower, so make sure that you strike a balance.

Only fools fall in love

Never fall in love with a project. The only consideration that determines whether you proceed with a deal is the profit number in your deal analyser. New developers can find themselves prone to wishing a deal would work because they've spent a lot of time on it. They know it would be a fantastic project. As a result, they don rose-tinted spectacles regarding their contingency, assumptions, and target margin. That's not relevant. Go with your standard assumptions and let the numbers guide you. Never let your heart rule your head in determining whether to go for a project.

Always target a 20%+ margin

Be aware that your commercial lenders will usually require you to target a margin of at least 20% (on GDV) before they lend. You should always reject deals that do not produce a 20% margin, minimum, in any event. Make it your golden rule. Never be tempted to accept a lower return. A 20% margin gives you a fighting chance of making a profit even if several things go wrong. More importantly, it means you will be better placed to repay the bank. Working to lower margins gives you far less comfort, and if things go badly wrong, you could make a loss. While a 20%+ margin doesn't guarantee profitability, it will place you in a much less risky position.

One point to note here is that as you progress through the number-crunching stages, your early numbers on any deal will involve a lot of assumptions. **You don't have to be returning 20%+ at every analysis stage for a deal to pass to the next stage.** If the early stages produce a profit figure which is on the way to 20% but not quite there, the next stage may see that number improve as the numbers get firmer and the assumptions are replaced with quotes. The golden rule is NOT that you ditch deals that don't make 20% at first glance, only that you don't purchase a deal that doesn't return

20%+ profit. Clearly, some deals will be obvious no-hopers from the early stages, and so you can eject them from the funnel at that point.

Always factor in a contingency for unexpected costs

One of the critical risks associated with property development is unexpected costs. You can do all the due diligence you like, but when your utility company takes three months to sort out the gas supply, or your contractor discovers some air conditioning plant in the roof void, these costs aren't budgeted for. And the list of possible unexpected costs is virtually endless.

The easiest way to budget for these unexpected costs is to continue to make reasonable but prudent assumptions for the known expenses and then add a contingency for potential unknowns. How much should this be? A contingency of around 10% of the construction cost in property development is not unreasonable. You can afford to budget a lower contingency for conversion projects than if you were building new since there is less scope for unexpected costs (as you are not going into the ground).

When it comes to analysing deals, contingency is essential. Some people describe it as a buffer, a safety margin that means you've allowed for additional unexpected expenses without impacting your bottom line. We describe it as a cost and not a buffer. Why? Because while you don't yet know what the cost will be for, you are 99.9% guaranteed to have at least one unexpected expense hit your project. A buffer sounds like you've built some fat into the deal that you could potentially strip out if you need to make the numbers work. The reality is that you'll almost certainly be spending some of it.

So, here's one of the Golden Rules of development:

ALWAYS allow for a contingency and NEVER think of the contingency as an optional cost that you can strip out to make the numbers in your deal analyser work.

A word about block planning

A key factor you'll need to work out on any project is how many units you can fit into the site since this will determine your total GDV. The principle of block planning is very simple. You create a scale outline of the perimeter of your site. Then inside that perimeter, you draw in as many flats as you can reasonably fit, allowing for numerous factors, including:

- Access – you must be able to get to each front door without crossing anyone else's property or climbing across the roof
- Light – all your units must be able to have sufficient light coming into their living areas without overlooking other properties
- Cycle and bin storage – you need to allow sufficient communal space for bikes and bins
- Unit type – you'll need to know what mix of flats you're looking to build and the minimum size (floor area) of each type

We strongly advise that you take the time to learn how to block plan. It's a key part of our mentorship programme since, if you can accurately calculate the number of units you can fit into a site, you can initially appraise a deal without asking your architect to do the block planning for you. This saves both time and money and makes you much more efficient at analysing deals.

Ignoring the asking price

The asking price of a piece of land or a commercial property is simply a 'hope' price. It represents the maximum price the agent or the vendor thinks (or hopes) they can get for the property. It's not necessarily the only price they will accept.

You should never make the asking price a factor in your initial calculations. Always start with the highest GDV you can realistically squeeze from the deal, deduct 20% profit and then deduct your best estimate at the cost of delivering the project, i.e., construction costs, fees, and finance costs. What remains is the maximum you can afford to pay for the property. If you now compare this to the asking price, you can get a steer as to where you're likely to stand regarding the vendor's aspirations.

Freehold considerations

When you build a house or a block of flats, you have a choice of selling them leasehold or freehold. A freeholder owns the property and the land, whereas a leaseholder owns the unit internally (but not the structure) for a fixed period but not the land on which it's built. Leases can run for various periods, usually between 21 and 999 years. Most flats in the UK are leasehold, and this enables the freeholder to charge the leaseholder an annual ground rent, effectively a small rental fee for the land that the flat sits on. It's not a huge amount; typically, around £250 per annum. At this rate, a block of 20 flats would produce a ground rent income of £5k per year to the freeholder. However, the longer-term benefit for the freeholder is that the property reverts to them when the lease expires. In our example, if the freeholder's 20 flats were on 99-year leases, then having sold the flats today, they could collect £5k per year for the next 99 years as ground rent and then resell the flats at the going market rate in 99 years. In reality, the leaseholder will most likely strike a deal with the freeholder when there are 80-99 years left on the lease to renew it.

There is an active market for trading freeholds, with many businesses making a living from the ground rent income from owning a significant number of freeholds. However, in February 2022, the Leasehold Reform (Ground Rent) Bill 2021-22 was passed into law, which restricts ground rents on newly created leases of houses and flats to an annual rent of one peppercorn (a token of no financial value). This means that new leases are no longer likely to have any significant value to freehold purchasers. While this could be viewed as lost income for the developer, the reality is that it will add value to new flats which are sold freehold (instead of leasehold), so the developer should command a small premium as a result.

Making offers early

If all your initial due diligence is looking positive, you now need to consider making an offer, something that can strike fear into the hearts of novice developers! When you're buying your own home, making an offer feels like a significant commitment. After all, you're making an offer because you've decided you want to live in the property. This decision usually hinges on the property's features, feel, and location rather than its price. We don't usually buy somewhere to live simply because it's great value. Therefore, when we make an offer, we're usually committed. We're at the equivalent of stage 4 in our deal analysis funnel.

With development opportunities, profit is the only consideration. You're not going to live there, and you only want to complete the project so that you can make money. Any offer you make is non-binding and will always be subject to your due diligence. If it subsequently transpires that the opportunity is unviable financially, then you'll be withdrawing your offer. The agent and vendor may be disappointed, but unlike a home purchase, they know that the deal has got to stack up financially for you to go through with the purchase.

By making offers early, you're putting yourself forward as a serious buyer. You're not going to be offering on every deal you look at. But once you've got to a point where a deal is looking reasonably good at stage 3, an offer will get you an inside track with the agent and allow you access to more information.

Many new developers tend to want to get to stage 4 and quadruple-check every single number before they make an offer, by which time it's often too late. So, always consider an early offer if your numbers are looking good, even if there's quite a lot of firming up still to do.

If you've got a decent relationship with the agent, then an offline conversation about an offer can be helpful. Rather than making a formal offer, you say something along the lines of: "Let me tell you where I'm at. I can get the deal to stack, but only if I secure the property for £200,000. I know it's below the £250,000 the vendor is looking for. Is it worth me putting in an offer at £200k, or am I simply out of the running at that price?"

This informal approach allows you to sound out the agent WITHOUT making a formal offer. Their response could be that an offer at your proposed level is way off beam, in which case you'd probably walk away. On the other hand, the agent might say that the vendor won't accept £200k but might be interested at £220k. The point is you'll get some form of response from which you can gauge the level you should be going in at and, therefore, your next steps. It also avoids making an embarrassingly low formal offer by email and looking like a chancer; at least you've taken the trouble to explain where you're at, even if your number isn't where the vendor might want it to be. You've not made an offer, but you've got a steer as to where you lie in the game.

So, we've now covered the key concerns that most prospective developers worry about. We've talked about:

- How you can look credible even when you're brand new to development
- How and where you can obtain finance from
- The best places to look for deals
- The importance of solid deal analysis
- Making offers early and firming up your pricing assumptions

In the final part of the book, we'll be looking at what it takes to get started as a developer.

Part 4

Developing Your First Project

14. Could YOU Take On A Small Development Project?

What does a successful property developer look like?

In theory, property development is open to every adult, irrespective of their age, gender, nationality, experience, or skills. But aren't there are some characteristics that define the more successful developers, even if we're only talking about small-scale projects?

Well, that's a very good question, so well done for asking it ☺. In response, let us share with you those skills we believe you'll need in order to be good at development, and then we can talk about those attributes that make some people more successful at it than others. But first, we'd like to explain why being a good property developer is similar to being a good CEO. In other words, you're the top dog, you make stuff happen, but most of the work is done by other people. Oh, and you get the biggest pay check of the lot.

Interestingly, the role of CEO has a job description all of its own, and to some extent it transcends the industry. Yes, the CEO needs to know about their market sector, but the day job is fundamentally the same regardless of the industry they're in. It's one reason why we see 'professional CEOs'; people who have gone from running one type of business to another, in completely different sectors. You might recall a chap called Adam Crozier, who started out as CEO of Saatchi & Saatchi. He went on to became CEO of the Football

Association, Royal Mail, and ITV, and has also been Chairman of Whitbread, Vue Cinemas, ASOS and BT. All very diverse businesses, but the same skills were needed to run all of them.

We often use the role of a cabinet minister as another example, specifically when a cabinet reshuffle is on the cards. One day the right honourable member enters Number 10 as the Health Secretary and emerges half an hour later as the Defence Secretary. On paper it's a bizarre appointment. The top person now in charge of the country's multi-billion-pound defence budget knows nothing about defence at all, having only that morning been on the TV announcing a new round of NHS cuts (or spending, depending on your optimism). It doesn't make sense. Yet the reason behind their appointment lies not in their technical knowledge, but in their skills as a politician. They are the CEO of a government department, and the skills they use are the same regardless of the department they run. Yet within their new department they'll have an army of people that live and breathe defence. They know it inside out, and it's this team of civil servants and officials who will be briefing the new minister. Sure, the minister needs to know their high-level stuff, but they'll be reliant on the team beneath them for the detail.

In both examples, the role is analogous to that of a property developer. You play the lead role, but you have a team around you who have the necessary technical knowledge to deliver what needs to be delivered. And the skills you bring to the party are not property development skills specifically; they are the basic entrepreneurial skills needed to run a business.

So, what are those skills? There are four that we consider to be critical:

People skills – you'll need to go and talk to a range of professionals to shortlist and then appoint them. You'll also need to be in touch with the key members of your team during the project's build phase and will need to both communicate with them and maintain each relationship. You'll also have relationships with commercial agents, residential agents, brokers, commercial lenders, and private investors.

Management skills – you'll have to be able to give your professional team some form of instruction and manage the business plan for your project.

Organisational skills – you'll have to make sure that you've got the right people in place and that things happen in the correct order without missing out any critical steps.

Decision-making skills – when your professional team asks you to make a decision (usually with their guidance), you have to make it quickly and decisively.

The interesting thing about all these skills is that most people already have them, despite never working in property development before. That's because they're generic. In fact, most people use these skills to some degree in both their day job and in everyday life.

As we've already mentioned, the role is very similar to that of a Chief Executive Officer or CEO. You've got overall responsibility for everything, but it's other people who do the physical work, and you just facilitate that.

And as you've probably already worked out, that's why the name of our business is called propertyCEO.

The success attributes

So, if you've got those four basic skills then you're going to be in a good place to move forward as a developer. But if having those skills is a pre-requisite, what are the attributes that differentiate a good developer from an average one? The good news is that, having trained many prospective developers, we've compiled a list of the factors we think are likely to make you more successful. So here goes:

Being pro-active

At its heart, property development is an entrepreneurial craft. Yes, it's a role that countless people have performed previously, but ultimately nothing happens unless YOU make it happen. In fact, it's one of the rewards of creating new homes; you know that they simply wouldn't have existed without you doing what you did. Like a proud parent, you brought a home into this world and it will (hopefully) still be standing long after you're not. Applying the same proactivity to every task that you do will always set you apart; it's way too easy to be complacent.

Going the extra mile

This is arguably the biggest factor in any new developer's success, particularly when it comes to finding a project. You've heard us talk about how doing straightforward, small-scale conversion projects can produce substantial six-figure profits from an outlay of relatively little money in quite short timescales. It's not surprising, then, that you won't be the only person trying to get into this market. As a result, it's imperative you can differentiate yourself from the competition by getting educated and working harder and smarter than they do. This means doing more and going further. Many people bemoan that it can be hard to find a deal, yet they don't go about it the right way. They don't make enough of an effort to forge the right relationships with commercial agents, nor do they try and find direct to vendor off-market deals. Where everyone else is good, you need to be great. That way you'll differentiate yourself from the crowd and win deals.

Systemising as much as you can

While you can't systemise everything, you can systemise a lot. Things can get messy very quickly if you're not organised, and that just makes life difficult and costs you time. Start out with a plan to systemise as much activity as possible, and it will pay you back in spades later. You'll thank us for it, we promise.

Learning your craft

Some people have a notion that you can learn how to develop property by reading a book or watching YouTube videos. Just like any business venture, the people that invest in their education before they get started are nearly always more successful. In development it means knowing how to win more deals and make more money, not just avoiding mistakes. There are a lot of people who try their hand at development without getting educated, and there are also plenty of experienced developers who only know what they know, and miss tricks left right and centre. Being educated allows you to leapfrog these people and put yourself in a much stronger position.

Being tenacious

It's easy to get disillusioned, particularly when you're struggling to find deals. Successful developers understand that it's this struggle that makes the competition cave in and walk away. As long as they stick with it and keep going, they will find a deal. The first deal is the most difficult one to find, and you only ever fail if you give up.

Walking a mile in someone else's shoes

Property development is a people business. That means you must deal with lots of different people who each do different things and perform different roles. It can be very easy to think only about what these people can do for you. However, we've found that the most successful developers take the time to understand the world from other people's perspective. Work out what other people want or need from you, and you'll help them. Then they become much more likely to help you. This is particularly true when it comes to visiting your own site. When you see your contractor's labourers and workpeople working, take the time to introduce yourself and find out how they are. Is everything ok for them on the site? These are the people that are building your project plus they're the ones that will find practical solutions to problems when they crop up. Be aloof or ignore them, and they're not going to think twice about not going the extra mile or finding a cheaper work around. Be a decent, civilised person who's grateful to have these skilled people working on your site and you'll find it can go a long way. Oh, and bringing some coffee and doughnuts along once in a while probably wouldn't kill you ☺.

Being permanently glass half full

Property development can be a bit of a roller coaster ride, with ups and downs all over the place. The trick when faced with a 'down' is to be annoyingly positive and upbeat. Even if your initial reaction is to throw someone into a skip, instead smile outwardly, tell yourself that there's a solution out there somewhere, and that you just need to jolly well go and find it. Infect your team with the same level of enthusiasm, and you will go far.

If only there was a tried and tested system

The McDonald's fast-food restaurant brand is one of the most widely recognised in the world, serving around 70 million customers every day and employing over 200,000 people globally. The golden arches have grown to become a symbol of western culture across the globe, and the business generates over $20 billion in revenues each year.

Given its success, those who aren't familiar with the brand's business model may be surprised to find that a significant proportion of its restaurant managers are relatively young, often in their teens. With the average restaurant turning over half a million pounds a year, why would such a successful brand have such young and inexperienced people heading up the restaurants that are at the heart of its business?

The answer to that question underpins the single biggest secret to McDonald's success. Which is that McDonalds isn't a group of 40,000 independently operated restaurants run under the same brand. It's a single business system that delivers one product solution to its customers through 40,000 outlets.

The key to any business lies in its systems and processes. Ray Kroc famously worked out that the most effective way of serving fast food to customers was to deliver a single product experience to every customer. It gave him huge economies of scale, and the 'streamlining' production method created a production line that was easy to replicate and easy to follow. It also meant he wasn't reliant on key individuals to be able to deliver his product; the system took care of almost everything.

Regional variances aside, you can go into any McDonald's in the country and receive exactly the same experience, from the service you receive to the food you consume. Restaurant managers aren't able to decide how long to cook the fries for or what specials to put on the menu. Nor can they decorate their restaurants differently or use a different brand of toilet roll in the rest rooms. Everything is a prescribed process, and all an employee needs to do is follow the system. Which is why it's possible for McDonald's to employ teenagers as managers. They're not having to rely on employees' personal restaurant management experience to make them successful. That experience is instead embedded within the system's processes, and all the employees need to do is follow them.

Now, we hope we haven't just alienated our fast-food management readership, as we're not for one moment suggesting that running a restaurant of any size or description can be done without any initiative, skill and responsibility: far from it. There are plenty of important variables that aren't covered by the McDonalds training manual, like customers for one. But the point is that if you have a business with well-documented and prescriptive processes and systems in place, then life suddenly becomes a lot simpler. And invariably the business becomes more profitable and a lot easier to manage.

Ritchie has run many businesses during his career and quickly worked out that most can be distilled into 8 key areas. It didn't matter what the business did, how big it was or what market it operated in, 8 was always the magic number. Unsurprisingly, property development was no different, and one of our key objectives when we sat down to devise propertyCEO's training was to make sure that our students can follow a straightforward system. We called this system the 8 Pillars (because we didn't want to overthink the title), and it follows the journey of a new property developer as they tackle their first project. It effectively gives our students a road map that makes their journey a lot easier. So, we thought it might be helpful to give you a high-level overview of these 8 Pillars, so you can see the batting order:

Pillar 1: Credibility & Brand

It all starts by making sure you look like a competent professional before you do anything else. 'Only fools rush in' is the quote and never is it truer than with development. In Pillar 1 you create your brand and make every aspect of your fledging property development business look professional. This is such an important element that we even appoint our mentorship students with a branding coach so that they can look like a million dollars before they've started.

Pillar 2: Business Plan & Structure

Our business coaches work with students on two key areas. The first is making sure that they have a suitable business plan; one that represents their business well and that can be used as part of the day-to-day operation of the business. There is zero point having a business plan sitting in a drawer gathering dust.

The second element is getting the structure of your business right. We've talked about some of the structural options and considerations earlier, and you'll have gathered that it's critical to get things set up correctly right from the start as very often you're not able to undo things if it subsequently transpires you could have paid less tax.

Pillar 3: Professional Team

As you will have gathered, your team of professionals is one of the key components of a successful property development model, and it's vital that you do a good job of recruiting great people. This is the next step in the process, making sure that you've already established your brand in Pillar 1.

Pillar 4: Finance

With money being the lifeblood of any deal, it's amazing that you can get so much financial leverage in the development world. The fact that you can effectively borrow all the money you need to and only pay any money or interest back once you've sold out and your profits are in the bank is incredible. But it still requires you to get this finance in place, both with commercial lenders and private investors, and this is what the fourth pillar is all about.

Pillar 5: Deal Sourcing

Deal sourcing is where your systems can really come to the fore, plus you should be able to outsource some of the workload to other people such as an assistant (virtual or otherwise). This includes building those all-important relationships with agents as well as exploring options for finding off-market deals.

Pillar 6: Deal Analysis

Once you've found a deal, you need to have total confidence that your numbers are correct. Making sure that you not only have the right deal analysis spreadsheets and tools set up, but also that you have a process for firming up those numbers as a 'sales funnel', getting rid of non-stacking deals as you progress rather than attempting to fully analyse every deal.

Pillar 7: Technical & Planning

Here we are mastering our knowledge of the planning system to make sure we have the best possible strategy and are looking at opportunities that we can progress with speed, certainty and of course, profit. You would also be covering subjects such as health and safety and making sure that you know your legal requirements and obligations as a developer.

Pillar 8: Project Control

This is arguably the most important pillar, because if you get it wrong, it can undo all the good work you've done in Pillars 1 through 7. Pillar 8 is all about delivering the project on site and making sure that you end up with some profit to show for your efforts. However, it isn't about project management; that will be the job of your Project Manager.

Getting help when you need it

Having a system is great, but property development is not a colour by numbers exercise. There are few straight lines to follow because every project is different, often in many unique ways. As a result, you can follow an underlying system, but eventually you will encounter issues that sit outside the training manual, particularly when it comes to the detail. There will be a thousand little nuances (and possibly several big ones) that you've not encountered before, and so you're not necessarily going to know exactly what to do. Wouldn't it be a disaster if you did most things right but then made a rookie error because you came across a new problem for which you didn't have the right answer?

First things first, you're an entrepreneur, and for entrepreneurs there's no detailed roadmap to success. If there was, it would be something that everyone would be doing because they could just follow a process and be successful.

The key to being a successful entrepreneur lies not in having all the answers yourself, or by making ballsy decisions based on your gut feel. The key is to know how to find the solution or best guidance to any problem you encounter, and then make a decision based on best information available. And being a property developer is no exception.

Your expert resources

So how can you get to a position where you have access to the best advice on any solution you may need? Let's look at your resources:

Your education

The simple fact is that the more knowledge you have, the less help you're going to need from other people. We'll talk about education in the next chapter, but ideally, you'll not only want access to comprehensive information, but you'll also be able to refer to course materials at any time you need a refresh – with lifetime access for preference.

Your professional team

It's incredible that we can recruit a team of people that have such a diverse range of expertise and technical knowhow. Whatever your question, you should be able to find your answers simply by reaching out to your team, particularly where it relates to a specific discipline or where it's a question relating to a technical issue.

Your Project Manager

Your project manager is a real blessing since, unlike most other members of your team who are masters of one specific area, the PM can see the bigger picture. They will act as your eyes and ears on the ground and should be one of the first people you would turn to for guidance or advice.

Your NEA

One of the unique benefits of having a non-executive advisor on board is that they can advise you in your role as a business owner and CEO. Whether it's advice on dealing with a particular challenge or issue, or simply running an idea or decision by them, they can be invaluable. Another key advantage is that they may be able to spot things that aren't on your radar and act as a second pair of eyes on your business.

Your own common sense and gut feel

Property development isn't rocket science. At its heart, we're doing something very simple, namely sticking some materials together to create a building. Yes, there are many technical aspects, particularly when it comes to the detail but, as the CEO, you don't usually need to worry about these as they'll be well-covered by your team of professionals. So, when you're faced with a decision, a crossroads, or a bump in the road, you can usually rely on your own logical reasoning, common sense, and gut feel to give you a sensible way forward.

A word about risk

One of the primary objectives of any property developer should be to eliminate as much risk as possible. You want to be in a situation where your realistic worse-case scenario is that you fail to make a profit. You never want to be in a situation where you lose money. And while it's not possible to guarantee you won't, hopefully you'll have recognised that a significant part of what we've spoken about in this book relates to the reduction and control of risk.

So, your key take-aways from this section are that a) there IS risk in property development, and b) that you CAN do a lot to reduce it. As a reminder, here are the ways in which we advocate you reduce your risk exposure:

- *Get yourself educated*: an obvious point, but clearly if you know what you're doing then you'll have de-risked your position considerably
- *Avoid planning risk*: by choosing PDR schemes you avoid much of the risk associated with the planning system. Also

make sure you have a good planning consultant on your team

- *Keep projects small*: if something goes wrong on a small project, the impact is usually less painful than on a larger one. Plus, smaller projects tend to be less complex, and therefore less risky, logistically. And you can still make a healthy six-figure profit from a small scheme

- *Always target a 20% margin against GDV*: that way you can afford to have some things go against you and STILL come out with a profit

- *Appoint an NEA*: having someone on board who can assist you in getting your first project across the line will be invaluable – and could prove priceless

- *Avoid heavily contaminated sites*: old petrol stations and the like can look interesting and appear good value, but they could all too easily hide a big problem

- *Appoint a health and safety consultant*: since this is a key legal responsibility, make sure you get this right

- *Always have a minimum 10% contingency built into your numbers*: you should always assume that you WILL spend it

- *Firm up all your pricing assumptions before you buy*: don't get lazy and assume that 'ball-park' will be close enough

- *Use commercial finance*: so that you get an independent assessment of your project's viability

- *Avoid JV partnerships*: unless you're very, very sure it's the right thing to do

- *Use separate limited companies (SPVs) for each project*: so that any problem in one project won't affect any of your others

- *Always have two exit strategies*: if you're building to sell, make sure you have a plan B that involves keeping the units and renting them out. And if you're building to rent, your plan B option should involve selling the units instead

- *Have a system for everything*: the more you systemise your business, the less risk you'll overlook or miss something important

Hopefully you're beginning to build a picture of what's involved in development and whether it's something you could take on. We've explained that this book isn't designed to be a development 'handbook', rather it's a starting point for deciding whether development would be a strategy you should consider. So how do you go about finding out exactly HOW to develop property?

For that, you'll need to get yourself educated, so that's where we'll be heading next.

15. Getting Educated

You don't know what you don't know

As you will by now appreciate, property development is a complex business. And while you can do a lot to reduce the amount of risk involved, you can't remove it altogether. While it's reassuring to know that you have a professional team around you to take care of most of the technical stuff, it's you who's ultimately taking all the financial risk here.

One of the challenges we regularly see is that the barriers to entry for new developers are very low. This is a key attraction for many people since it compares extremely favourably with other professions. For example, if you want to earn a six-figure salary as a dentist, you can't just buy a fancy chair and a spittoon and set up shop in your dining room. You're first required to get a degree in dentistry, which takes five years, and then you must complete two years of supervised on-the-job training. Even then, you're only likely to make £30-40K as a junior dentist. In fact, the average salary of a UK dentist is just over £51k, according to Payscale. So, if you want to make a decent six-figure salary, you need to be running your own practice. Not only does that require a whole host of different business skills, but you'll ideally have to build up your reputation as a dentist for a few more years before you can start. And then, of course, you need to make your new practice big enough and successful enough to pay yourself a six-figure income from it.

Compare dentistry to property development, and the differences are stark. There's no need to take a five-year degree course and have on-the-job training. And even doing a small project should net you a six-figure return. Your team will be able to draw on a whole range of technical skills as trained experts in their field, but none of these skills needs to be learned by you as the developer. And as a result, you can get started straight away and be enjoying your new six-figure income within a couple of years. You don't even need to be doing it full time so that you can keep your day job! No wonder then that many people see property development as an easier route to financial success. The fact that you don't have to look in people's mouths all day is just a bonus.

Now, this won't come as a massive shock to you, given that we run a property development training company, but we think it's critical that you get trained BEFORE you tackle a development project of any size. So, having declared our interest, let us explain why we think it's such a good idea, and you can then form your own view. Because, unlike dentistry, getting trained in property development is optional, so it's entirely your choice.

Let's start with some basic facts:

You don't know what you don't know

This is arguably the number one trap that new (and sometimes not-so-new) developers fall into. Put simply, if you don't know a hole exists, how are you going to avoid falling into it? There are so many holes you could potentially fall into as a developer. And because we're talking about projects involving six and seven-figure sums, the impact of a fall can potentially be life-changingly bad. We don't understand why people would knowingly want to risk so much, but we guess some people might think, 'how difficult it can be?'. Perhaps they can imagine the end-to-end process of building a house; surely their professional team takes care of all the complicated technical stuff? In any event, can't they just pick things up as they go along? That's what they've done in their other businesses. And maybe they'll be lucky and avoid all the holes!

If this is your line of thinking, then we're afraid you're in for a nasty shock. Property development isn't easy, and we've had the pleasure of educating numerous developers who decided to go back and get trained AFTER they fell down the holes. You see, even with some experience under your belt, there are plenty of undiscovered holes left for you to find.

Risk is money

If you don't know what you're doing, you have a much greater chance of getting into difficulties. The investment you make in getting educated will pay you back many times over. It's simply a false economy not to. It would indeed have been cheaper for Sir Edmund Hillary to have said, 'let's ditch the Sherpa and save a few bob', but would anyone genuinely have thought it would have been a great idea?

Sh1t will happen!

No two development projects are the same, and there are many moving parts. Similarly, no single development has ever progressed to completion without some hitch or other occurring along the way. It has simply never happened. And the downside could mean reduced profits or even losing money. Being educated won't guarantee you'll never lose money, but it can help you avoid many of the pitfalls.

Seeing opportunities

But only half of the benefit of being trained properly is avoiding pitfalls. The other half is about teaching you where to see opportunities that others can't see. We've talked about the places where you can find opportunities in this book, but there are many more. You need that 'edge' to win deals and maximise your profits, and that's what proper training can give you.

We're genuinely bemused that anyone would think it's a good idea to enter a highly competitive market like property development without knowing a) where the pitfalls are and b) where the opportunities are. What sort of business strategy is that? What competitive edge do they think this arrangement gives them when competing against both experienced developers and new developers who <u>have</u> been trained? Can't they see that this logically makes them the people least likely to succeed?

You may have heard of the expression 'standing on the shoulders of giants'. In other words, we see further not because of our own stature but because we borrow the expertise of those that have gone before us. And that, in a nutshell, is what educating yourself is all about.

The infamous training pyramid myth

We often get asked whether someone can become a property developer straight out of the box when they have no prior property experience. This question usually comes from people who've been told that they need to start with a buy-to-let or two first to build up their property confidence, experience, and knowledge. Once they've done that, they can maybe move up to some HMOs. Then they could graduate to some 'advanced strategies' such as serviced accommodation or rent-to-rent. Only once they've worked their way up the property strategy 'pyramid' are they then deemed 'qualified' enough to be able to tackle something as big and complex as a development project which sits proudly at the top.

This argument is like saying that to learn to drive a car, you must first start on the pavement with a skateboard before moving on to a scooter and then a pushbike. Then you can take your pushbike on the road before stepping up to a moped and then a motorbike. Only then will you be able to learn to drive a car.

In other words, total rubbish. If you want to develop property, go ahead. Many landlord developers we know started owning rental property <u>after</u> they became developers. Given that you need more capital to become a landlord, doing it this way makes perfect sense – it's the profits from developments that allow many people to start their buy-to-let portfolios. Otherwise, you could end up learning how to be a landlord and then realise you haven't got a big enough deposit to get your journey started. Presumably, you'd end up needing to follow another strategy that will enable you to make enough cash so that you can pursue your first strategy. It all seems back to front if you ask us.

Does this mean that there's zero commonality between development and other property' strategies? No, they're all businesses that involve property. But, as we've already seen, the process of creating a small-scale development project is very different from that of being a landlord. Experience as a landlord will be as much use to you as a developer as development experience would be to a first-time landlord. In other words, some benefit, but not a huge amount. They're simply different business models that have property as their base; one is not a more 'advanced' version of the other.

How much should you pay for your education?

Another frustration of ours (we have to say this chapter is proving remarkably cathartic) is that there are people who say that you don't need to spend a lot of money on training to be a property developer. We recently heard this from a chap who was selling a £300 property development training course. Technically, this is true, in the same way you don't need a parachute to be a skydiver. It doesn't, however, mean it's a good idea.

To give some perspective here, we can share that our flagship six-month mentorship programme would set you back a low five-figure sum, while we also have some intensive workshops that are in the low four-figures. Given the gulf between this and a £300 workshop, how do you know the right price to pay for training?

One way could be to contrast it with training costs in various well-paid professions. For example, in the medical profession, it costs around half a million pounds to train a GP, and they will go on to earn £100,000 per year on average. There are no official stats, but we'd expect a successful small-scale developer to make at least that, and potentially quite a lot more. How much, then, should a developer pay for their training if they can make more money and do it more quickly? £1million? £100,000? We don't think so. But then we don't believe that £300 is the correct number either. Even a three-year university degree course in most subjects typically costs £27,000, and the chances of earning six-figures any time soon are fairly remote (the average graduate salary is around £24,000 at the time of writing).

Perhaps the entire world is missing a massive trick? Maybe you really can learn how to do development safely and successfully by reading a free e-book, spending £300 on a half-day training session, and then go and earn six figures next year in your spare time without making any mistakes. We don't think you can, but we DO believe everyone is entitled to their opinion.

There you go, rant over. In summary, if you're serious about doing development, our recommendation would always be to invest in decent training; ideally, the best quality training you can afford. It will genuinely give you the best possible chance of success and of minimising risk.

The jam tomorrow dilemma

When considering any training, one of the challenges is that you ideally need to do the training BEFORE you start doing whatever you're being trained to do. It would be far handier if you could earn six figures from your first development and then use it to pay for the training afterward, but that's not the way life works. As a result, people are faced with the prospect of shelling out for training today and then having to wait for their labours to bear fruit before their training investment is repaid.

There's also a question mark hovering in the air somewhere. After all, it's one thing planning to try your hand at property development but pocketing the proceeds from your first project is another thing altogether. So, if you buy the training, will you go on and make property development become a reality? It's certainly not guaranteed.

So, what's the solution. Well, the honest answer is there's no real shortcut. The best training will get you the best results, but it usually costs the most money to buy, and the best time to buy it is before you start. Which doesn't solve the problem.

It does, however, lead us to make a further recommendation. Do not spend a load of money on property development training until you are sure you want to become a developer.

Which is where we may be able to help.

We decided to do several things right at the beginning when we first launched propertyCEO. The first was to create the best property development training product on the market that was also the best value. Modesty aside, we think we can justifiably say we've succeeded. However, we were also passionate about making sure people understood what was involved in property development BEFORE they invested a load of money in any training (ours or anyone else's). After all, it would be easy to sell people a dream about making serious six-figure profits working part-time. But property development isn't simple, and we wanted people to understand precisely what was involved from the outset.

As a result, we developed a range of training materials designed to educate people about development, warts and all. We created books, videos, articles, speaking events, webinar shows, and online training workshops, all aimed at delivering this fundamental level of education to people, so they understand what's involved in development without having to shell out loads of cash. We make all of this information available for as close to free as we can make it (apologies if you paid for this book, but you can take some comfort in the fact that any profit we make from it goes to charity – thank you! ☺).

Providing free training admittedly sounds like a rash move on our part, from a business plan perspective. But the simple reality is that we have no interest in selling courses to people who are chasing a dream because many of them would be unsuccessful. Far better that every student we take on knows what's involved, has confidence that they can make it happen, plus WE have confidence in THEM. That's why you can't buy our mentorship programme online; applicants first have to be interviewed by us and invited to join the programme.

If you want to soak up all the free stuff, please head over to www.propertyceo.co.uk – it's all accessible through the website. Although (spoiler alert), we may be offering you a sensational reader-exclusive training offer in the next chapter, so you may want to wait a bit.

The questions you need to ask

Finally, in this chapter, we've put together some thoughts on the due diligence you should do when looking for a trainer or training company. There are many training options at various price points, so please, please, please, do your research BEFORE handing over your money to any training company, ourselves included.

Here are the top 10 questions we think you should be asking when checking out the credentials of prospective trainer(s) and their organisations:

How much experience in development do they have?

A depressingly large number of trainers go on a property training course, do their first development, and then start trying to flog their own course. Ideally, you want to be working with people who have real-world experience and plenty of it.

What is their track record?

Get them to share some success stories and speak to some of their students. Are they as good as they say they are? Do they have multiple testimonials from current students? All training courses sound marvellous on the website, but the proof of the pudding lies in the feedback of those trained.

What is their current role?

Are they property developers who run a training business as a sideline, or is property development training their main thing?

You want to have confidence that they've real-world experience of doing what they're training you to do. But what if their main priority and focus is their own development projects rather than their students? There's no right or wrong answer, but we'd say be wary of training where it feels like a side-hustle to someone's main business.

Who will your trainer(s) be?

Many training companies use their founders to promote their courses, but juniors or third-party trainers do the actual training. This isn't automatically a bad thing; providing your trainer has the necessary skills, experience, and knowledge to do the job well. If they're simply reciting what they've been told to say parrot-fashion, then there's almost no added value. Teaching property development isn't just about reciting facts; you need trainers who can use their experience to answer your questions. So, find out exactly who will be training you before you sign on the dotted line.

How much 1:1 time will you get?

"Mentoring" has a variable meaning in the world of training. In its purest sense, mentoring involves spending some serious time working one-to-one with a mentee. However, it has almost evolved to include any training where there is any one-to-one contact at all. At its least generous, this could be a monthly 15-minute phone call with a junior trainer, which can be hugely frustrating if you've got lots of questions or if the trainer can't answer them. Have an idea of how much one-to-one time you feel you'll want, and then get clarity on the course's mentoring level, expertise, and scale.

Do they have a helpdesk?

How do you pose any questions you might have while on the course, and what are the turnaround times? You want to email in questions and get answers on a timely basis. Do you get the impression that there's a dedicated support team in place and that customer support is a priority for the business?

How thorough is the training?

This can be tricky to establish because when someone says their training is 'comprehensive,' it doesn't mean very much. Far too many training products are heavy on the sales pitch and light on content. In development, it's the detail you want to know, so see if you can find a prospectus or agenda for the training. A professional-looking prospectus is a sign that they're invested in their business and that the quality of their materials is up to scratch. Also, see if you can find reviews or testimonials of people that have completed the course. Someone could sell you a £300 course that covers 'every aspect of development', but if they only dedicate five minutes to each aspect, then it's not going to teach you very much.

Do they have a 'sales funnel' model?

Many training organisations have a sales funnel where they get people to sign up for a free or inexpensive product and then upsell them to the next, more expensive product. Then, they simply rinse and repeat, so customers are sold increasingly expensive products or courses. You often find in this model that a lot of effort goes into the upselling since this is what drives the revenue. You'll receive some high-level content and then a compelling sales pitch for the next, more detailed (and more expensive) training.

There's nothing wrong with this per se, except that the number one focus of these companies is how to generate more sales revenues and not how to create successful students. You've also got to ask why they're not selling you the training you need at the outset rather than making you buy course after course. Tell-tale signs of this structure are when you keep getting upsold to a 'better' product tier (and there are lots of them) and when it feels like the last half of each training tier is spent trying to tempt you to buy the next one. Usually, you only find out about their best product is by working your way through their sales funnel, so why not just ring them up instead and ask them what the deal is?

In the interest of transparency, we have a sales funnel of sorts here at propertyCEO, but it's oriented slightly differently. There are many ways people can find us, but in almost every case, they will receive free and/or low-cost training initially. That's because we commit to making sure people understand whether development is a good fit before they can get invited onto our mentorship programme. Beyond the free stuff, at the time of writing, we have a 3-day online workshop for those that are seriously considering development and want to learn the basics initially, and then our flagship 6-month Mentorship Programme for those looking for the whole nine yards, where we work with them to make it a reality. We also offer an intensive 4-day in-the-room workshop where we follow an actual development from start to finish.

Do they specialise in the training you want?

Some training companies offer lots of different training products and strategies, while others specialise in one area. There's nothing wrong with either approach, but we'd recommend ensuring you're being trained by people who specialise in what you're looking to learn.

Do they offer the training format that works best for you?

The training medium has got to work for you. For example, do you prefer home study or seminars/workshops? You also need to decide whether you're looking for some high-level training, or do you want the more intensive, mentorship-type approach? The latter is more expensive but offers a level of support you won't get with the volume-training products.

Our advice is to do your research and ask around. It can be a bit confusing if you're new to it all, so we did a podcast episode on the subject of property training which you can access from our website www.propertyceo.co.uk/podcasts. In fact, there you'll find dozens of podcast episodes covering all aspects of property development, so please feel free to dive in.

We also host a free weekly webinar show called Open Door where we interview the movers and shakers in the world of property development and have a bit of fun at the same time. You can register to join the next Open Door on our website and check out the previous shows on our YouTube channel.

16. Next Steps

Where do you go from here?

In this book, we've hopefully whetted your appetite with the current opportunities in development, the system you can implement to take advantage of it, and of course, the not insubstantial rewards it can lead to. But we've also made a point of mentioning the risks and workload involved in making it a success.

Whether we've made you think twice about tackling a development project because there's more to it than you thought, or we've given you impetus and confidence to take things further, then, either way, it means we've done our job.

That said, there's a limit to the amount of information we can convey in a book this size. And even if you've been paying attention all the way through, you may not yet have enough knowledge to know whether development is a good fit for you, which is fair enough.

And so, we decided that, as you've bravely soldiered through to the final chapter, the least we could do is offer you a small parting gift by way of a thank you. In short, we'd like to invite you to attend one of our online training events as our guest. If, having read this book, you're still interested in development but want more information before deciding whether to jump in, then this free online training session is a good next step. So, if you can bear the thought of experiencing us train in person, simply go to:

www.propertyceo.co.uk/book-training-offer

This link should then take you to a booking page where you can see all the gory details and book your place on the next available training session if you'd like to. Since we don't know exactly when you'll be reading this book, if you find that the link doesn't take you where you were expecting, please go to the propertyceo.co.uk home page and follow the training links from there (and if you're reading this any time after 2032, you may want to consider buying the latest edition, as this one's at least a decade out of date, you cheapskate ☺).

The spotlight analogy

There's one final point we'd like to make about property development, and it's an analogy we often give to our students. Development can look like a complex beast with many moving parts. However, as the developer, you will never be focused on ALL of these parts at any one time. Instead, you will only be focused on whatever specific part of the journey it is that you are at right now. It's like having a spotlight shining on you. As your development journey progresses, so the spotlight moves along to the next part of your journey, and you only need to focus on what's in the spotlight. Too often people worry about how much there is to learn on the whole journey, yet they are easily able to master the actions they need to take that sit within the spotlight.

And finally...

We've made a point of giving you some tips about finding a good training partner in the previous chapter. Hopefully, you've gained a flavour of what we're all about from reading this book, but just in case you're interested in having us teach you, here's a list of ten things that we think are important. If you believe they are important too, then we could be a good fit for each other, in which case we'd love to try and help you:

1. We aspire to excellence in whatever we do. We genuinely want to make the best products and training materials that exist. We can't guarantee that we'll always get there, but that's what the sign says above the door, and we always try our very best to live up to it. That goes for everyone in the team. In short, we always aim to exceed our students' expectations

2. We don't try and hard-sell our courses. If you enjoy the hard sell experience, plenty of others out there can offer this service. Just don't all rush to the back of the room at once ☺

3. Property investment and development is a business, and too many people fail because they had a dream but had no idea about business. All of our training courses include an element of business training as standard so that we can do our part to make sure you stay in business

4. Most people operate at a fraction of their potential because, without realising it, they go through life with the handbrake on. So, we also include mindset training as standard so that you can achieve your goals more quickly. Practical things that you may not know about but which can make your goals much more achievable. Seriously, the mindset stuff just works – you should check it out if you're not there already

5. We specialise in what we do. We're not trying to become a training brand that offers a zillion and one different courses. So, we'll only teach you about what we know a lot about, not what we think might sell well

6. We'll teach you how to develop property, full stop. You might then decide to pursue a specific strategy or type of project, but ultimately, you'll be learning from us how to develop ANY project. There really are lots of different opportunities out there you could be looking at

7. Experience counts for A LOT in both business and property, and neither of us are what you'd call fresh out of college. We promise to aim for wisdom, but if we miss, at least you'll get experience

8. We don't outsource our training to third-party trainers. We have a team of professional coaches who specialise in key areas and who interact with our students on that subject. But the core training, the workshops, and the Q&A sessions are hosted by yours truly

9. We think it's important to give something back, which is why we host the podcast, our Open Door sessions, and also provide training, all for free.

10. And maybe above all, propertyCEO is also about having some fun along the way. Life's too short not to enjoy it. If we can help you become financially free and find the life of your dreams, then if you can enjoy the journey too, you've been our perfect customer

We wish you every success with whatever you decide to do next, and thanks for stopping by – we hope to see you again.

Ian & Ritchie

Alresford, June 2022

Appendix 1: List of Use Classes

GUIDE TO THE USE CLASSES ORDER IN ENGLAND (FROM 1ST SEPTEMBER 2020)

USE CLASS UP TO 31 AUGUST 2020	USE CLASS FROM 1 SEPTEMBER 2020	USE
A1	F2	**ASSEMBLIES | LEISURE | LOCAL COMMUNITY USES** Shop less than 280sqm mostly selling essential goods, including food and at least 1km from another similar shop.
A1	E	**COMMERCIAL | BUSINESS | SERVICE** Shops, retail warehouses, hairdressers, undertakers, travel and ticket agencies, post offices, pet shops, sandwich bars, showrooms, domestic hire shops, dry cleaners, funeral directors and internet cafes.
A2	E	**COMMERCIAL | BUSINESS | SERVICE** Financial services such as banks and building societies, professional services (other than health and medical services) and including estate and employment agencies.
A3	E	**COMMERCIAL | BUSINESS | SERVICE** Cafe or restaurant, for the sale of food and drink for consumption on the premises - restaurants, snack bars and cafes.
A4	Sui Generis	**SUI GENERIS** Drinking establishment, public houses, wine bars or other drinking establishments (but not night clubs) including drinking establishments with expanded food provision.
A5	Sui Generis	**SUI GENERIS** Hot food, takeaway, for the sale of hot food for consumption off the premises.
B1a	E	**COMMERCIAL | BUSINESS | SERVICE** Office other than a use within Class A2.
B1b	E	**COMMERCIAL | BUSINESS | SERVICE** Research and development of products or processes.
B1c	E	**COMMERCIAL | BUSINESS | SERVICE** For any industrial process (which can be carried out in any residential area without causing detriment to the amenity of the area).
B2	B2	**GENERAL INDUSTRIAL** Use for industrial process other than one falling within class E (previously class B1) (excluding incineration purposes, chemical treatment or landfill or hazardous waste).
B8	B8	**STORAGE OR DISTRIBUTION** This class includes open air storage.

GUIDE TO THE USE CLASSES ORDER IN ENGLAND (FROM 1ST SEPTEMBER 2020)

USE CLASS UP TO 31 AUGUST 2020	USE CLASS FROM 1 SEPTEMBER 2020	USE
C1	**C1**	**HOTELS | BOARDING | GUEST HOUSES** Hotels, boarding and guest houses where no significant element of care is provided (excludes hostels)
C2	**C2**	**RESIDENTIAL INSTITUTIONS** Residential care homes, hospitals, nursing homes, boarding schools, residential colleges and training centres
C2a	**C2a**	**SECURE RESIDENTIAL INSTITUTIONS** Use for a provision of secure residential accommodation, including use as a prison, young offenders institution, detention centre, secure training centre, custody centre, short term holding centre, secure hospital, secure local authority accommodation or use as a military barracks
C3	**C3**	**DWELLING HOUSES** Uses as a dwelling house (whether or not as main residence) by a single person or by people to be regarded as forming a single household of not more than 6 residents.
C4	**C4**	**HOUSES IN MULTIPLE OCCUPATION** Small shared houses occupied by between three and six unrelated individuals, as their only or main residence, who share basic amenities such as a kitchen or bathroom.
D1	**E**	**COMMERCIAL | BUSINESS | SERVICE** Clinics, health centres, crèches, day nurseries, day centres.
D1	**F1**	**LEARNING | NON-RESIDENTIAL INSTITUTIONS** Schools, non-residential education and training centres, museums, public libraries, public halls, exhibition halls, places of worship, law courts.
D2	**Sui Generis**	**ASSEMBLIES | LEISURE | SUI GENERIS** Cinemas, concert halls, bingo halls and dance halls.
D2	**E**	**ASSEMBLIES | LEISURE | COMMERCIAL | BUSINESS | SERVICE** indoor sport or fitness, gymnasiums, indoor recreations not involving motorised vehicles or firearms.
D2	**F2**	**ASSEMBLIES | LEISURE | LOCAL COMMUNITY USES** Hall or meeting place for the principal use of the local community. Indoor or outdoor swimming baths, skating rinks, and outdoor sports or recreations not involving motorised vehicles or firearms.
Sui Generis	**Sui Generis**	Use classes which do not fall within the above specified classes.

Appendix 2: Key PDR Classes

KEY PERMITTED DEVELOPMENT RIGHTS

Note: This appendix list some of the more useful PDRs for small-scale development projects and is not designed to be an exhaustive PDR list. Be aware that each PDR will contain specific terms and conditions that must be met and will require prior approval from the local planning authority; please consult the General Permitted Development Regulations for full details. Always consult a professional planning consultant before making any financial commitment or making planning applications that involve a PDR.

PDR CLASS   DESCRIPTION

ADDING NEW STOREYS TO AN EXISTING BLOCK OF FLATS
Adding up to two new storeys to a purpose-built, detached block of flats. PRIOR APPROVAL

ADDING NEW FLATS ON TO EXISTING COMMERCIAL OR MIXED USE BUILDINGS
New flats on detached buildings that are either commercial or mixed use with flats. PRIOR APPROVAL

NEW FLATS ON TERRACED BUILDINGS IN COMMERCIAL OR MIXED USE (SHOPS AND FLATS)
New flats in the airspace above terraced buildings (including semi-detached buildings) in commercial or mixed use (including residential). One storey may be added to single storey buildings; or two storeys may be added if the existing building is two or more storeys tall. PRIOR APPROVAL

NEW FLATS ON TERRACED BUILDINGS USED AS HOUSES
New flats in the airspace above terraced houses (including semi-detached houses). One storey may be added to single storey buildings; or two storeys may be added if the existing building is two or more storeys tall. PRIOR APPROVAL

NEW FLATS ON DETACHED HOUSES OR BUNGALOWS
Building additional flats on top of either detached houses or bungalows – so flats on a house in the airspace! PRIOR APPROVAL

DEMOLITION OF BLOCK OF FLATS OR B1 AND REPLACE WITH FLATS OR HOUSES
Demolition of either a single purpose built detached block of flats or a single detached building within B1 Use Class and it's replacement with either a single propose built block of new flats or a single purpose built house with up to 2 additional storeys for the new structure in the airspace. B1 includes offices and light industrial. PRIOR APPROVAL

USE CLASS E (COMMERCIAL BUSINESS & SERVICE), BETTING OFFICE, OR PAYDAY LOAN SHOP TO MIXED USE
This includes adding to flats above each commercial unit providing the upstairs is ancillary to the commercial space below. PRIOR APPROVAL

CERTAIN USES TO RESIDENTIAL
Allows betting offices, payday loan shops, hot food takeaways or launderette to be converted to residential, up to 150 sqm. PRIOR APPROVAL

BARNS AND AGRICULTURAL BUILDINGS TO RESIDENTIAL
Agricultural to residential, up to 5 units but not in a conservation area. PRIOR APPROVAL

COMMERCIAL TO RESIDENTIAL
Any use within the Commercial, Business and Service use class (E) to residential (class C3), up to 1,500sqm. PRIOR APPROVAL

Printed in Poland
by Amazon Fulfillment
Poland Sp. z o.o., Wrocław

25946665R00163